ONCE UPON A CHARIOT

ONCE UPON A CHARIOT

*A true story about Norma Jean Belloff,
who established the USA Women's Record
for Cross Country Bicycling in 1948*

WRITTEN BY IRIS PARIS

TATE PUBLISHING *& Enterprises*

Published by Tate Publishing & Enterprises, LLC
127 E. Trade Center Terrace | Mustang, Oklahoma 73064 USA
1.888.361.9473 | www.tatepublishing.com

Tate Publishing is committed to excellence in the publishing industry. The company reflects the philosophy established by the founders, based on Psalm 68:11,
"The Lord gave the word and great was the company of those who published it."

Book design copyright © 2008 by Tate Publishing, LLC. All rights reserved.
Cover design by Lindsay Behrens
Interior design by Jonathan Lindsey
Back cover photo by Deborah L. Horst
Published in the United States of America

ISBN: 978-1-60604-788-0
1. Biography & Autobiography: Sports   2. Inspirational: Motivational
09.04.28

Was the Lord displeased,
Or was Thine anger against the rivers,
Or was Thy wrath against the sea,
That Thou didst ride upon thy horses,
And Thine chariots of Salvation?

Habakkuk 3:8 (KJV)

This book is dedicated to

Lance Paris.

Contents

PROLOGUE
About the authors

Norma Jean Belloff was born in New London, Connecticut, on March 14, 1927. Second of four children born to a Navy man, she moved frequently. The main places she grew up were the Hawaiian Islands and San Diego, California. She graduated from Point Loma High school and attended San Diego City College until she married Berdine Harold Rogers at the age of twenty-three. Together they raised a son, Blake, and a daughter, Iris. Norma remained a full-time homemaker until her death at age forty-four. She was an active volunteer in the League of Women Voters and Red Cross Swim Program. Besides bicycling, she enjoyed botany, the Spanish language, painting, swimming, singing, and acting.

I, Iris Paris, was born in Fort Morgan, Colorado. My younger brother, parents, and I lived in Denver until I turned nine. Our family relocated to San Diego, and I lived there for twenty-eight years. My career in education began at age twenty-five, after I earned an Associate of Science Degree in Early Childhood Education. I taught and directed pre-school until I had my first daughter. After the birth of my second daughter and divorce from their father, I relocated with my two girls to Oregon in 1989. I attended OSU and earned a BA in Psychology, then an MAT in Education from Willamette University. I taught school for ten years in a variety of private and public settings including Linn

Benton Community College and Western Oregon State University. After retiring in 2006, I moved to Crawford, Nebraska, bought a fixer house on a hill, and painted it purple. I love to learn, laugh, dance, sew, hike, decorate, cook, and volunteer in both my church and community. Recently I have begun playing percussion instruments. Writing is another new adventure for me.

ACKNOWLEDGEMENTS

I did not write this book alone. It reached completion only because of the dozens of people who assisted in many different ways. First, I wish to express gratitude to Lance Paris, who did not let me quit, no matter what. I also thank my two beautiful daughters, Gemma and Julia, who have been neglected but still appreciated throughout the process of writing the book. My brother Blake Rogers and his wife, Valerie, gave me permission to share very personal details about our family in this book; I thank them both. I thank Beth Gibbons for her support and excellent detailed critique of every chapter.

Thanks goes to Ann Warren Smith, my writing teacher, who believed this book would be published shortly after I began to write it. I also express appreciation to my writer's group in Oregon, which included Karen Caswell, the encourager; Diana Hall, freelance editor; Linda Lawrence who asks direct questions; and Ruthanne Dean, my personal cheerleader.

Also, I thank for their encouragement Debra Stevenson; Jo Robertson; Sheila and Bruce Robertson; Roberta White; Dan Reyes; Pastor David Kennedy and his wife, Karalyn; and Pastor Marsha Stauss. I am grateful for interviews with Jamie Robertson on issues of young love and Mrs. O'Leary for detailed information about Texas, as well as many others too numerous to list here. Finally, I thank Dale and Donna

Steineke for their kind hospitality at their Ponderosa Ranch and for helping me realize when the story was finished.

Bless you all forever.

Iris Paris

Author's Preface
By Iris Paris

Until recently, my mother's accomplishment remained one of our family's best-kept secrets. The only visible clue during my childhood was a mysterious red racing bike, forever collecting dust in our garage (I recently learned that this was the last bike she owned and the one she used to take third place in the Women's National Bicycle Race Competition in 1948). The story of my mother's journey remained locked in the hearts of certain family members until 1989. Just a few weeks after I had relocated to Oregon with my two young daughters, my aunt delivered five trunks full of documents to my doorstep. Included in the delivery was my mother's trophy. Was I surprised and slightly irritated! Why me? My aunt assured me that they were part of my inheritance from my recently deceased grandmother. Thirteen more years passed before I acknowledged what God required of me—to write my mother's story.

Her true story reflects the optimism, passion, and faith of a young woman who dares to fulfill a dream she had begun when she was six years old; to bicycle across the United States alone. In the post World War II era, she set out alone to satisfy her curiosity about people and places beyond her everyday experience. In the process she established the women's record for cross-country bicycling—New York to San Diego in fifty-three days.

This story also depicts a bright and sensitive young

woman's journey of self-discovery, self-understanding, and self-forgiveness. My mother searched for answers. How could she love and accept herself and her imperfect family? During a time of increased opportunity for women, what contribution might she make to the world? She discovered America and thousands of Americans discovered a bit of it with her. She found that God was everywhere and was much more caring than she had known before.

As much as is possible, I have used my mother's own words, as found in her diaries, journals, and newspaper articles, which documented her trip. While all the events and people in this story are real, I took the liberty of embellishing dialogue, when my mother did not provide it. The information presented in this book is, to the best of my knowledge, the truth, and the message she sends is clear. Life may not always be beautiful, but it can be a beautiful ride. Human beings in their imperfection can certainly seem demonic; but by looking for the good in everyone, we will draw closer to God, our perfect Creator, and we will find the good we seek.

Sadly, my mother succumbed to mental illness by the age of twenty-eight. I was four years old when her struggle began. Eventually she took her own life at the age of forty-four. I was nineteen years old at the time of her death, the same age that she was when she started her wonderful adventure. I would not wish this loss on anyone. Unable to help her in life, I help her now by telling her wonderful story of exploration, forgiveness, and hope. It is with great respect and joy that I share my mother's journey with you. May it bless you as much as it has me.

Me, Norma Jean Belloff

Older Brother, Don, and I with our washerwoman and friend, Rose. Mt. Hope, Panama. 1929

My family and I leaving Hawaii upon my father's retirement from the Navy. Next stop, San Diego. 1940

Buddy and I at our home in San Diego as we depart on our trip to Los Angeles. October 1945.

Buddy and I on Thanksgiving Day, 1948, posing in our formal dining room, which Mother had lavishly decorated with fruit from our expansive garden.

Chariot I and I leaving home in San Diego. January 19, 1947.

Chariot II and I in Houston, Texas. May 1947.

My roommates and I in front of our boarding house in New Orleans. June 1947.

Me at Lake Ponchartain Amusement Park. New Orleans.
June 1947.

Chariot II and I just after release from Pensacola jail. I'm wearing the offending sunsuit. July 1947.

I discovered while on the East Coast, as I lounged at the beach, strangers often wanted to take my picture, and the boys flocked around me like flies. July 1947.

Grandmom in her garden. Baltimore, MD. April 1948.

Chariot III and I in our winter "togs." Baltimore, MD. Spring 1948.

Otto Eisele and I, Spring 1948, in New York.

President Truman and I finally meet in San Diego, September 1948, while he is campaigning for election.

(photo courtesy of San Diego Historical Society)

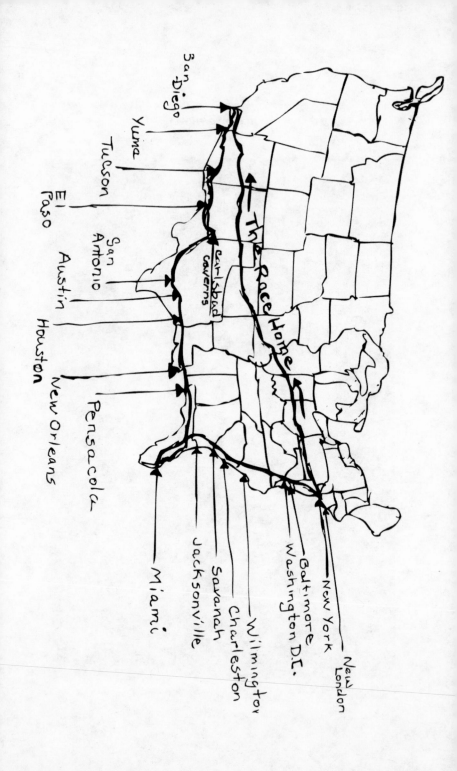

CHAPTER I
Almost Home

August 1948

My mind races as my legs pump and the ground flies beneath me. The scenery moves by like so many feet of paper on my mother's player piano, rolling, playing, and measuring my progress. Draped across my chest for the last fifty-one days, my slightly shredded *New York to San Diego* banner still flaps in the wind as I ride. In fact, all five feet, seven inches of me feels pounded and toned. I've lost twenty pounds since I left New York; there's not an ounce of fat left on me.

Now, as I pedal along Highway 101, south of Los Angeles, my sea-blue eyes water from the sting of the bright sun and persistent coastal wind. Squinting, trying not to think, I wail out another tune my mother taught me... . "I love to go a wandering along the mountain track, and as I go I love to sing, my knapsack on my back, Valerie, Val era," serenading the golden grass hills.

Around, around, around, the wheels of my sleek, black Schwinn Continental bicycle still purr. Though the chrome fenders of my *chariot* look brown with dust collected over the last three thousand miles of travel, mostly on Route 66, the gears still shift smoothly as I pass through small towns. Dotting the California coastline like lighthouses to the travel weary, the hamlets provide food, water, and temporary diversion from my discomfort.

The last one-hundred and fifty miles of my race stretch, interminable. The repetition of scenery seems two-dimensional now except for the smells ... cow dung, clover fields, and chimney smoke. Occasional whiffs of car exhaust mingle with the odor of diner-food cooking. My sun-tanned hands feel glued to the handlebar grips, stuck there with white-knuckle determination and sweat. Yet, I'm happy for a moment not to know where cycling ends and my life begins. Like a merry-go-round, I think. I never want to get off.

"Life is miraculous!" I'm twenty-one and still alive, though many times I could have died. "Thank you, God, for your blessings!" I shout toward heaven. In spite of this prayer, other thoughts creep in, uninvited. Almost two years have passed since I've seen my family; father, mother, sister, and two brothers, and so much has happened.

"Buddy has run away again." I can still hear my mother's worry-worn voice when we spoke on the phone, just last month. This was not the first time my sixteen-year-old brother had disappeared for long periods. Occasionally, the world just swallowed him up.

Mother's words spin round and round in my head and anger re-fuels my will to pedal, rather than walk, up the steep and winding hill I'm climbing. Why had he run away this time? Will I ever be able to help those that I love the most? With each stroke of my legs, I release emotional pain. Pushing against injustice, massaging my grieving soul, my screams exit my toes and blow away with the wind.

Holding my breath, moments pass; then unable to resist, I suck in the warm summer air like a newborn babe taking its first gasp. The race continues and cannot stop. I have a record to set. Besides, if I stop I might smother in my sense of helplessness. "Then you, Norma Jean Belloff, will be no good to anyone," I say to the cows lined up along the white wooden fence on my left. Tossing my head in defiance of their complacent stares, I shout, "They say life's a bit like pouring water in a Coca-Cola bottle. If you're the least bit scared, you just can't do it!" Ha! Ha ...

Miles later, I glance to my right to see the summer sun setting, catching the Pacific Ocean on fire. My lanky limbs feel scorched. I wear only a skimpy two-piece sun suit again today. My tangled blonde hair is, I'm sure, bleached a shade lighter. You've got nothing on me, Marilyn Monroe. A chuckle gurgles its way from my gut to my lips but doesn't quite escape.

Minutes later, "Okay, I give up!" I say to the silhouettes of sea gulls flying by. Seventy miles of pavement have flown beneath me after another day of cycling America's highways, and I'm one day closer to setting the first ever United States record for Women's Cross-Country Cycling.

Screech! My trusty chariot moans as I brake to a stop for the night. Chariots I and II had been clumsy and heavy compared to the racing bike I now dismount. My first steed, a single-speed, balloon-tired touring bike, had held up admirably ... until I lost it in the Colorado River. Right now, I especially miss its extra-wide cushioned seat!

Feet and legs aching, finally too tired to think, I toss my worn sleeping bag down behind a protective clump of Laurel Sumac bushes, just a few feet from the roadway, and crawl in. I don't even bother to unload my Bible from the back of my bike.

My stomach full of burgers and fries I'd wolfed down in the last coastal hamlet, the musty smell of sage soothing my chafed nose, I find bliss in instant deep sleep. Dreaming, I'm an infant again, without sin. Safe in my mother's arms, she rocks and sings to me. I sleep, as at the end of hundreds of other days I've traveled, knowing that tomorrow will have troubles of its own, but it will also have a purpose. I rest well, nestled in the hope of God's supernatural and everlasting mercy, and in the mysterious knowledge that, with His help, even my wildest dreams can come true.

CHAPTER 2
The Beginning (One and one-half years earlier)

January 1947

Is God laughing? I wonder as I stand silent, grinning sheepishly at my mother. The irony is that I secretly long to bury my face in the soft folds of her neck and weep, saying, "Please don't send me away!" The familiar scent of lilac talc mixed with dirt from her precious garden would comfort me. All this pretending! This is how it is in my family. Ironic that Mom, who lives so carefully, could launch me off on a ten-thousand mile cycling trip, my ultimate destination, Baltimore, Maryland, where grandmother lives, then back home again. Mother shows no concern about it at all! "I'm sorry for being so selfish, so bratty, and so disrespectful," I long to say. My heart aching for forgiveness, for her to beg me to stay.

Instead, I say, "Thank you for the Bible, Mom. I'll clamp it to the carrier on the back of my chariot and read it every day." My *Chariot of Salvation*, a phrase borrowed from Habakkuk in the Old Testament, is a heavy, balloon-tired, single-speed Schwinn bike that I had purchased with twenty-five dollars of my own hard-earned money. I knew that my racing bike wouldn't hold up as well on the bumpy roads that I would be traveling for the next year or so.

Whose idea had this trip been, anyway? I thought it was mine but, looking back, it seemed like Mom was practically pushing me out the door! In October 1945, she and Pop had allowed my brother Buddy, then thirteen, and I, eighteen and a senior at Point Loma High School, to cycle together all the way to Los Angeles. What mother in her right mind would allow such a thing?! At the time we had actually felt lucky to have such a *liberated* Mom. Mother said she was teaching us to trust in God. The truth is that both of us had been skipping school a lot and many saw us as both social and academic failures, opposites of my younger sister, June, and older brother Don.

The plan had been for me to continue across the United States to visit relatives in Baltimore while Buddy cycled back home alone. The problem was that I got so homesick, I just couldn't do it. Besides, I felt that I was deserting little Buddy in more ways than one. Then there was my guilt about leaving Neill, my off-and-on-fiancé. Oh, my! Buddy and I returned home together after two weeks.

Today dawns and seems like any other. By the time I get up, the frost has melted, and downstairs a huge breakfast of eggs and cow brain with sliced avocado and toast on the side waits (Mother is convinced that eating brain increases our intelligence). Pop is already at work, teaching large-engine mechanics classes at San Diego City College. My brother Don, the oldest and smartest, is away at college. Juney, my *precious* little sister, off to school. Buddy is *who knows where* ... again.

Denial can seem like such a good friend. None of them had said goodbye. They didn't want to wake me, I imagine. Maybe they pretended that it was a normal day, and that they would see me in the evening. Perhaps they would miss me too much to think about it; I hope this is true. Then there is Neill. After giving him so much, I purposefully neglect to tell him I'm leaving. My heart twangs with regret for things left unsaid to all of them. Yet, I leave.

Butterflies tickle the inside of my stomach as I recheck my bicycle loaded with only the bare necessities. Sleeping roll, change of clothes, towel, hairbrush, toothbrush, lipstick, canvas tarp, tool bag, flashlight, canteen, and my new Bible. A large sack lunch Mom carefully packed sits on top of the rest. Twenty-five dollars, wrapped in wax paper, is hidden inside my brassiere. It's all I have.

Golly! There isn't a cloud in the San Diego sky; the winter sun is already weakly warming the crisp air. I inhale deeply, all the scents of home. Will other places smell different? Mom pretends to examine one of her beloved tangerine trees for frost damage. We both know we will not see each other for more than a year. I memorize her standing beside me in her matronly housedress and kitchen apron, graying brown hair pulled up and back in a practical bun, her jaw set in that determined way she has.

"I'm ready to go, Mom," I say as I mount my *steed*.

"Call me tonight if you can, Norma," she says. Her pale blue eyes moisten as she gives me a quick hug. "Remember, if you need money, I can wire it ahead to wherever you'll be staying." I avoid her gaze as stubborn pride fills my heart. I've already told Mom that I didn't intend to ask for any help from her or Pop.

Finally, wearing my favorite plaid flannel shirt, blue jeans, and Keds, I begin the greatest adventure so far in my nineteen years of life on earth. Pushing off and coasting down our short driveway, then peddling down the gravel alley bordering one side of our expansive two acre estate, it occurs to me that I could just peddle around town and be back by nightfall! Tour San Diego or see the United States. Yet, as I head out for Highway 80 I know in my heart that I won't return to my home for a long time. I remind myself that this is about being free to do what I want. The world beckons. I answer the call. But, who am I trying to fool? The truth is, I'd heard Mother's convicting loud sighs one too many times, when I lounged uselessly around the house or gallivanted with my bicycling buddies instead of finding a job or marrying Neill.

The final big hint came several months ago in the form of a note, conveniently left on Mother's kitchen desk. Listed there in perfect cursive were all the costs my parents accrued for supporting me in their home. Food, cloths, medical and rent. I know if I don't leave now, my parents will *lay down the law*; grow up or move out. I feel squeezed hard from both sides like an annoying pimple, so, with arms opened wide and knees knocking, I embrace my destiny; Grandmom's house or bust. Though I've only met Grandmom twice, I know she cares for me in a way my mother never could. At Grandmom's house, good things will happen.

I make a beeline for the huge weight scales wharf-side of the ferry in San Diego Harbor; upon recommendation from some of my *know-it-all* male racing buddies, including Neill. Chariot and I weigh a total of two hundred fifteen pounds; sixty-five of it is Chariot and belongings. Neill would chide me for thinking that I could make good time with this kind of a load. He's already warned me that women should not travel alone. I think he's jealous; wishing he could come with me instead of remaining strapped down by college courses and his parents' expectations.

San Diego was much smaller before the war. Now the whole city is still bustling, though the war ended over a year ago. Downtown literally squirms with all kinds of people. Though camouflage nets no longer form a protective canopy over Pacific Boulevard, and sugar and butter are back on our family table, the streetcars and buses are packed with people in military uniforms. Pop said the war was good for our town. He calls it a good war. How can a war be good? Perhaps it is easy for him to say since neither he nor Don nor any of our friends or relatives were injured or killed in it. I don't dare ask questions. Questions make him holler!

Other questions burn holes in my brain. Does it bother our neighbors that my father is German? I'm embarrassed to say that last year I told my teacher my ancestors were really from Russia and then pointed to the town on the map of Russia named *Belloff*. And another thing. Both Mom and Pop warned me to stay away from downtown and sailors. Why? My father and older brother are both sailors. Why does Mother often cry quietly as she tends her garden? Is it for the dead that she weeps? Why? Why? There are so many things that my family refuses to discuss. I hope the world will be less secretive. *Whoosh.* I release my frustration to the wind as I glide forward.

Riding through Mission Valley is easy. Though there is some traffic on this two-lane highway, running east and west through San Diego County and beyond, the slope is gentle and the view picturesque. I ride *no-hands-on-handlebars* most of the way. Heading east, on my left side dairies spread, surrounded by green fields dotted with black and white cows, the San Diego River drifting small and lazy down the middle. On my right, steep slopes tower, specked with boulders, sage, and tiny winter wildflowers. The sun shines brightly now and warms me so that I remove my Pendleton and tie it around my waist. This is what it's all about—the sights, the smells, and the freedom. Excitement ripples through my body, and my pedals fly under my feet. *Swoosh. Swoosh.*

Winding my way for twenty miles into the foothills east of San Diego, I spend my first night in El Cajon Valley in the middle of an orange orchard. My green canvas tarp, draped over Chariot and me, conceals us from sight. The second night I sleep by the side of the road in Alpine—thirty miles today. By the end of the third day, I arrive in Descanso—twenty miles, all uphill.

I often get off to push my Chariot as I climb the west side of the Sierra Mountain Range. Enjoying the slow pace, I have time to examine the native plants, familiar to me from my extensive browsing of mother's worn copy of *Field Book of Western Wild Flowers* by J.J. Thornber. My legs are strong from all the cycling I'd done last summer, but I'm not in any hurry. This isn't a race. This is my life, and I don't want to miss anything. Besides, by taking the slow way across the United States, I'm buying time to figure out what I want. Perhaps I can delay the necessity of making difficult choices about what to do with the rest of my life!

"Mom, it's wonderful! You and Pop are darlings to let me do this! Sorry I didn't call sooner. I'm in Pine Valley, and I'm staying with Ken and Laura B. and their two little boys. We met at the local café, and they invited me to do some work for them in exchange for a spot on their couch. They feel like family after only two days."

"Norma, I'm so glad to hear from you! I pray for you

daily, and I know that you are safe in God's hands," Mom says, confidently.

"I filled their horse trough with water, one bucket at a time, in exchange for a ride on their horse and food. Tomorrow I'm off again for the last push over the coastal range. Next time I call you, I'll be in the Imperial Valley." I'm breathless.

"You should write to your friends in San Antonio to let them know you're coming," Mother warns. Is she worried? I hope so.

"Mom, the Bs asked me why I don't carry a gun! They think I don't know what I'm getting into. They're shocked that I'm traveling alone and are worried about what might happen to me. I told them, like you said, that a Bible is more protection than a gun. I said I was afraid that if I had a gun, I might shoot somebody!" We both laugh, and her chuckles sooth me. "Mom," I add, "you told me I would be safe … and I believe you." Silence hangs between us for too many seconds, then mother says, "That's right, Norma."

"Norma," she continues, "The *Ocean Beach News* will pay ten dollars per week for stories about your travels that you write and send to me." How dare she interfere! I stifle the furry rising in me and simply say okay.

CHAPTER 3
The Ups and Downs of Cycling the Sierras

January 1947

My feet sizzle! I long to kick off my Keds and pedal bare-foot, my favorite way. Climbing the last peak of the Sierra Mountains, I'm determined to reach the top before night-fall, on the fifth day of my journey. The scent of the scenery changed from pine to sage since leaving Pine Valley. The slope of the hill changed from gradual to grueling. The January sun feels like summer. I know the pavement will fry my soles; so, to distract myself from the discomfort of sweaty sneakers, I play the game of chasing my shadow on the road. As the day wears on, I occasionally stop to examine wildflowers or to dip my steaming tootsies in an icy mountain stream.

Slow, tedious hill climbing gives me time to think. Is it normal to feel shame all the time? Perhaps I was born ashamed. I'm not sure. When I was fourteen I found the definition of shame in the *Winston Dictionary for Schools* (1940). "A painful feeling that accompanies guilt. Guilt, the fact of having done a wrong. Sin." Sin. Right there in the dictionary!

I must be very guilty because, like a mangy street dog, shame sits outside the screen door of my consciousness every morning. Shame, so familiar, scratches and sniffs and whines until I relent and let it come in. Curling up comfortably on my lap, shame dominates my day. I can invoke shame from simple thoughts. A certain tone in my mother's voice, eating too much food while knowing that there are those in the world going without, remembering the look on Neill's face when I broke off our engagement, and thinking about leaving little Buddy behind. At still other times shame comes for no specific reason. He stays and stays and gnaws on old bones; memories I try to forget but can't. Let's face it. I'm doomed. I had never dared talk to anyone about these feelings. Even my one best girlfriend in my whole life, Jean—who I met in high school—didn't talk about these kinds of things. Would I meet someone someday whom I could trust enough?

I pedal even harder, retrieving myself from the bottomless pit of these depressing thoughts. My bottom throbs from constant contact with Chariot's hard seat. A few miles later, I feel bottomless! Numb in several places, all I can think of is to push and steer up the long, steep grade. I scour the ground ahead for obstacles—focusing on the rhythm of my pedaling. Eventually, everything else in my mind melts away like butter in a pan.

As in many times past, pumping with all my might, I melt into my bike. Lost in the popping and crackling of tires on the gravel shoulder, which vibrate through my body, I and Chariot are one. My soul feels cleansed for the moment. Tingle, tingle, tingle.

Now breathless, I gasp, steam escaping from my mouth like a locomotive ... I think I can, I think I can. I lean my chest forward on the handlebars; elbows thrust out like pathetic wings. "Why can't I fly?" Thigh muscles hard as steel, calves like rocks, I stand straight up on my pedals and inch forward. "Why do I seem to be standing still while cars zoom by?" My heartbeat pounds in my ears—*lub-dub, lub-dub*—muffling the sound of the offending engines.

I spy the hillcrest at last. Huge boulders, the color of cream, tower on either side of the road, framing the crisp, blue horizon. Have I reached the end of the world? The truth will soon be revealed. Just one more push. Hot trickles of sweat ooze from my pores, my mouth parched, as I finally dismount and push my leaden Chariot, drained of all emotion except a dogged determination not to slip backwards.

Suddenly, I hear the deafening roar of a large truck engine as it approaches from behind. No one's mother should know what I do next. With a mindless surge of adrenaline, I swing to Chariot's saddle, pump hard, and grasp an iron rail on the right side of the truck as it passes by me at a tortoise's pace. Swaying, shimmying at first, I finally find a balance between the dislocating pull on my left arm as I grip the truck and the unpredictable jiggle of my bike. My legs folded back, my thighs squeezing the sides of the seat, and my right hand alone on the handle bar, I cling with all my might.

What! Oh no! The truck, which I thought was an Angel of Mercy, turns instead into a roaring Devil as it threatens to drag me forward from my Chariot and crush me under its huge double wheels. Still I cling.

At the hillcrest, my left-hand knuckles freeze. I can't let go! Now, scenery zips by, nothing but a blur as Chariot begins to vibrate with too much downhill speed. "God help me, I don't want to die!" I scream and close my eyes for seconds. As if in answer to my prayer, Chariot's front wheel collides with an unidentified obstacle in the road; the jolt jerking my hand from its deadly grip. Chariot and I leap and land together. We screech to a wobbly halt as I slam back hard on the foot brakes.

Rattled but unharmed, I glance back up the hill, one hundred yards or so, to where I'd begun my dangerous descent. An unusual shaped lump at the top of the hill catches my eye. My sleeping roll had bounced from my luggage carrier and lay, forlorn, on the shoulder of the road, waiting for me to retrieve it. Should I? Of course I will in a few minutes.

Grateful to be alive to pedal another day, I have learned my first big lesson about risky behaviors on the road and I promise myself never again to hitch a ride of any kind, not even a tow by a burrow, for the rest of my trip.

The monstrous truck now looks as small as one of Buddy's toys, building speed as it descends into the great desert valley below. Did the truck driver know that I'd hitched a ride? Some questions may never be answered in this lifetime. At this moment, all pain is forgotten. I spy the expansive vista beyond the truck. The desert spreads out like a white and tan blanket, warming mother earth. Lines of smoky grey and pale brown mountains lay far in the distance, framing God's patchwork quilt.

"Yippee," I yell with all my breath, gasping to see the possibility before me. Startled by the sound of my own voice, I realize that I've not spoken for hours! Glancing quickly around to see if there are people who might think me odd ... silly me, no traffic. I lean Chariot against a bright red Manzanita bush, and, forgetting my exhaustion, I begin to stomp my feet, pushing defiantly against the pavement. Stomping and spinning in the middle of the road, head and arms flailing, I dance a *whirling dervish* of victory and jubilation. Free. I spin. Triumphant over what seemed undefeatable. I spin. "Oh, thank you, God. My God! I dedicate this dance to you." I spin.

It's strange how shame can *drop in* uninvited. This time it drops like a bomb on my joy, halting my dance abruptly as I think about Mom. She has to know about this immediately. Except for certain horrible parts. Panic strikes. No phones nearby. Urgency spurs me to flop down on the nearest semi-flat chunk of scratchy grey granite, pencil and pad in hand, and sketch what I see. Somehow I know Mother must see every detail so, in her mind, she can travel and be free too. Mountains, valleys, Yucca, and rocks emerge from my pencil to cover my small piece of stationary paper.

Are risk and freedom somehow connected? Could acts of risk and suffering help me escape from guilt and the relentless nagging of shame? Perhaps from sweat and sacrifice redemption would come as I ride on my *Chariot of Salvation*. But if shame left, what would take its place? What would redemption feel like? Who could tell me? Oh, sometimes I wish I didn't have a brain!

Tired of thinking, I warble "Somewhere over the Rainbow" in my best Judy Garland voice. My audience of attentive barrel cactus stands reverently still and bliss visits as the sun sets. No worries about spending the night by the side of the road in the middle of nowhere with no one but the rattlers, scorpions, and ants. Oh my.

CHAPTER 4
Surprises in the California Desert

January 1947

Next morning down the east side of the Laguna Mountains I speed, non-stop; a twelve-mile roller-coaster ride of a lifetime! Squinting to see the grey pavement through the blur of my watering eyes, I'm sure Chariot tops fifty miles per hour. I hope I won't collide with any large bugs or birds. If one of my wheels falls off or my brakes gave out, or if I hit even a small rock, like a human rocket launched on a final mission, I could become food for the ravenous turkey vultures when I land on the desert floor far below. Still I speed on, winding and twisting on the narrow, two-lane highway.

Half way down the mountain, my father's voice booms out from the recesses of a narrow canyon on my left as I whiz past it.

"Be careful, Norma, be careful! Do you have a death wish?" The voice echoes and seems so real!

"Don't turn your head to look," I mumble, "or you'll lose your balance for sure." Then, shouting backward, "Maybe. I don't know. Why do you care anyway?" Finally, "Right now, I don't care what you think!"

Perhaps it's my newfound feeling of freedom that makes me reckless. I thrive on the adrenaline rush of this risky behavior, just as when I hitched a ride on the truck. If my mother could see me now, it would probably scare her to death. Shame on me! Perhaps the gnawing of hunger and loneliness fuels my willingness to take bigger risks than usual. Nevertheless, with nothing but an orange in my stomach and a few hastily read words from the Scriptures in my head, on I speed.

Is this a test of my faith in God, or just a stupid, childish stunt? Could I out-peddle death? Young people are supposed to feel indestructible, aren't they? Life, after all, is a terminal condition. Better to die doing what I love than slumped in a rocking chair. So, racetrack-style, I bend my elbows, lean my chest forward to hug Chariot's handle bar, and pick up even more speed—compelled to careen to my destiny. Death or *El Centro*, which ever comes first.

The wide desert valley at the bottom of the mountain greets me, tickling my nostrils with the pungent odor of sage, moist from recent rain. The air feels twenty degrees warmer here than up in those mountains I'd left behind so quickly. Glancing ahead, I drool at the sight of the Chocolate Mountains. They stand, waiting for me, looking delicious and pastel on the far side of the valley. The road ahead wraps around them like a ribbon, tying the mountains into a yummy package. "Chocolate, Chocolate, I like chocolate," I chant in rhythm to my pumping legs.

The sleepy town of El Centro appears in the dusk. Civilization looks good to me after a few days of solitude. I stop at the post office where my first-ever-mail-from-home awaits me. Sent general delivery, the newsy note from Mom reminds me that *God travels with me*, and that money is just a phone call away. Thanks, Mother. Guilty again for no particular reason. I pedal, exhausted and starving, to a burrito stand farther down Main Street. I spend a precious quarter for the best burrito ever, not caring that the cook can't say, conclusively, what kind of meat it contains (dog?).

People back home had warned me that there was nothing in *The Center*, but I find it full of friendliness and activity. After looking around, I choose the Claude Vedder Trailer Court for my headquarters at fifty cents a night. Faye, the kindly manager, directs me to a space of ground among the trailers, near the office and her cabin, where she feels I'll be safe. She even offers me the use of her desk for writing and mentions the best places to eat in town. I think I'll stay here awhile!

January 25, 1947

I write to mother in the El Centro Public Library. I document my journey to send to her for publication in the *Ocean Beach News*. I'll include my sketches in the letter, but neglect to describe my descent into the desert; that's my good deed for the day. Inhaling the familiar, comforting smell of books reminds me of Mom's private library of carefully catalogued classics shelved in our den at home; Mom believes that every crack in one's soul can be patched up with a book. Obediently, I had read most of her collection before I turned seventeen. I feel better.

By the time darkness falls, I leave. A few yards from the library door, Chariot leans chained to a lamppost, waiting for me. When I squat down to unchain him, I don't believe what I see. My tire pump and rear valve core have vanished and Chariot's back tire sits flat as a pancake! Fresh scratches and dents mar the metal around the tail reflector where vandals had tried to remove it. Who could be so mean? "Everything happens to poor little me," I moan, dramatically, hopping around like the betrayed Rumplestiltskin.

Gaining some composure, I remember what I'd read

in *Nancy Drew*; criminals often return to the scene of the crime. Determined to get my revenge, I cross the street and crouch on a bench in a mortuary garden, ready to pounce (even though God says revenge belongs to Him). The lights in the library go dark. Then into the lamplight from somewhere in the shadows steps a tall, lean man who strolls slowly towards my bicycle. I sneak quickly in a semicircle behind some bushes to leap out in front of my wounded Chariot. "Are you the one who stole my pump?" I demand, trying to keep my voice steady. The startled stranger halts abruptly in his tracks.

"I'm a fireman from the local station, just out taking a walk," he says, shrugging his shoulders as he looks me over. Stupid me!

"Sorry," I say, my face burning with chagrin. Without looking back, I quickly wheel Chariot away to a service station at the edge of town, for repairs. After pedaling back to the trailer court, I try to forget it all in sleep. This is the first time in my life that I've been robbed, and my sense of trust is wounded. Tears burn in the back of my eyeballs, but they don't fall. "Big girls don't cry," I hear my father's voice reprimand me.

Sunday morning, at the Baptist Church, Faye leads us in prayer to forgive the thief. My resentment lingers in spite of the prayer, but what else can I do? I still want revenge! After all, some say that revenge is an expression of a woman's grief. Aren't I grieving over a loss of trust and a wounded bike? Who can I punish for this crime? I feel inhumanly alone.

Raised by a *Baptist* mother and a *scientist* father, I seem destined to always be seeking the deeper meaning of things and to question anything I think is true. It's wrong to steal. Do I have to forgive someone even when they're in the wrong? Did I deserve to have this happen to me? I don't know!

Over-thinking things makes me restless, so after church, I hitchhike to a rodeo in Brawley, a small town fifteen miles north of El Centro. Leaving my troubles behind, I can only hope my precious bike will be in tact when I return. Grrrrr!

I love everything about cowboys. I learned about them by watching movies on the big screen, and this is my first chance to see some in person! They are already there when I arrive. I keep my distance, peeking sheepishly, overwhelmed with awe. Cowboys! Squatting in a row, leaning against the chute fence, they look to be some foreign tribe, trading tales and opinions while chewing on tobacco. Swearing drifts up and out from among them like a profane prayer. Smelling of horses and sweat, mystery surrounds them. How can they dare to ride bucking broncos with names like Red Angel and furious bulls that kick in rage at anything near by? Why do cowboys, often wounded and dejected from their falls, still return time after time to try again? These men must harbor unfathomable, indestructible secrets. What do they know that I don't?

Ruggedly handsome, the young *cowpokes* remind me of my little brother, Buddy. He would have squatted too, his face as brown, his body as lanky, and his boots as battered. Sometimes I feel motherly; full of pride and worry for Buddy's well-being. Is this a normal feeling for a sister to have for a younger brother? I wish I could give him a hug right now and tell him that everything will be all right.

I feel too shy to join the cowboy clan as they talk, so I climb up on the fence to watch the show, vowing to meet at least one cowboy before the end of my trip. This is a *Mom and Pop* rodeo held on a private ranch. Soon, cars arrive in billows of dust and line up around the corral fence to form the grandstand seats. As the events begin, the local wives pour coffee and open bottles of pop while the hot dogs sizzle; my stomach growls at the tangy smell of grease. The ranch owner's children bicker about which record to play over the loudspeaker. Other kids tear back and forth, showing off on their horses. A pretty sight it is, full of fun and family, and though I'm a stranger, I feel like I belong.

I've always hated the idea of a nine-to-five job. Perhaps I'm lazy at heart, or maybe working a *regular* job is a symbol of all that I loath. Whatever the truth, I need money; so I try my hand at packing lettuce at a plant in El Centro with Faye's friendly daughter. Refreshingly different than any work I've done before, I'm paid by the box! I can pack as fast or slow as I want. The trouble is trying to pack fast enough to make any money; we're only paid a few cents for each crate we fill. In the next three days, however, I should earn enough money to get to Tucson. Yippee!

February 1, 1947

I'm off, leaving behind a brokenhearted young surveyor, Sam, who I'd met at a café the second day in town. Sam proposed to me, today, on a whim. Wow!

"There's just something about a girl on her bike that makes me want to capture her and bring her home with me," Sam explained. A lot like my big brother Don, who I'd always had a crush on, this guy is older and wiser, serious, gentle, shy, tall, dark, and handsome. He has a good job, and he is available; two important requirements for a husband. He'd probably like to keep me barefoot and pregnant, and both of these conditions sound okay to me, but not yet. So I tell my disappointed admirer that my heart still belongs to Neill. This is true, even though I haven't written to him since I left San Diego and our engagement is off.

Continuing east, with money in my pocket, I eat fresh dates, picking them from the palm orchards, all the way across the Imperial Valley. Dates, dates, and more dates as I pass through many small towns; Holtville, Date City (makes sense) and Gordon's Well. Chariot and I zip by large irrigated fields of vegetables, many crops ripe for the picking in the middle of winter, no less! I understand more with each mile I travel, why all my experienced bicycling friends told me to go south as I travel east. Although it may be fewer miles to Grandmom's house if I cycled across the middle of the United States, the frigid temperatures this time of year could easily kill me. Yes, south is best.

None of this valley looks like desert because they irrigate with the precious water from the All American Canal, just west of Yuma. The canal looks refreshingly cool and harmless! Thinking I might take a dip I find the sides of the canal too steep for me to climb into. *Drat*! So as a fireboat passes, torching weeds along the edges, I flag them down and ask if I can take a ride. The men gladly oblige. They ask me about my travels and warn me that the current in the canal runs dangerously swift, even though the water looks placid. I'm so glad they told me! The boatmen guffaw as they dowse me with bucket after bucket of water from their hose at my request. A welcome reprieve from the heat, I scream with girlish delight thanking them profusely by giving them all wet hugs before I continue. What would my father think of that?

This is my fastest day yet; sixty miles in six hours. It feels like a San Diego summer as I pedal; gentle, warm wind caressing my face. After pondering the idea of spending the night in the sand dunes, I pick a pure white crest of the highest sand dune overlooking Beau Geste Valley for my *natural* hotel. Movie studios make their desert pictures here, I'd read somewhere. I wish I could magically transport my silly little *sis*, Juney, here to play in the sand with me. We could sure act out some wild stories.

Sis, you are my best friend ... when we're not fighting. We've lived through so much together. You look so different than me, with straight brown hair, caramel eyes, and skin several shades darker than mine. Sis, with round, plump body,—you remind me of an Indian princess. Like the myriad colors of tans and browns of the desert, God also creates his people in many different hues. Though we are often jealous of one another for this or that, the different color of our skin doesn't make you and me any less kin, or any more or less loved by God. Nor for that matter, any two people on earth!

The sharp evening shadows heighten the drama reeling inside my head. I lay Chariot down and cover him with a tarp for protection from the shifting sand, then prance along a wind-rippled hump of a dune until I find a steep drop. Down I tumble, head over heels, laughing insanely and swallowing grit. At the bottom of the hole I rest and hum the song that Juney had learned in grammar school. "Gallop My Charger." I miss you, Sis.

I read somewhere that hundreds of people come to these

dunes to play each Sunday. Today one set of footprints trails over the swells; a windstorm has swept my private playground smooth. I won't get lost if I follow my own tracks. As the winter sun sets, I settle into my sleeping roll for the night, eating dates and drinking long droughts from my canteen. Then I surrender myself to dreams.

I wake sometime in the night bathed in crisp moonlight. Eerily, the dune's hills and valleys appear flat, while shadows of high clouds create dark, symmetrical patterns on the shimmering sand. I rise sleepily and stride along, basking in the perfect silence, broken only by the occasional whistle of wind or the howl of a coyote. Whoa! I step off the top of a high dune into thin air and roll down its steep face. Topsy-turvy, I laugh loud at the trick nature played on me, then bury myself in the warm, silken sand.

Oh no! Hideous visions of the rattlesnake I'd encountered earlier today invade my frolic. Although dead on the road, the snake had appeared as big around as the upper part of a man's arm and lay longer than I stood tall! I shudder to think I share the desert with such monsters. Even though snakes are one of God's creatures, I can't appreciate them at all just now. It's amazing how a good dose of nature can remind me that I'm not invincible after all and that I'm not ready to be *terminated* yet. Back in my sleeping roll, flashlight shining, I devour some Psalms to remind myself that God is mightier than that snake; just as He had answered David's cries for protection, He hears me. Overflowing with awe of all God's creation I join the coyotes and wail out a midnight prayer. "Our Father who art in heaven ... Amen."

Chapter 5
More or Less in Arizona

February 1947

I read somewhere that life is both more and less than what we hope for, but I rebel against the idea. God, I want it all! Neill, athletic, intelligent man; you were more than my seventeen-year-old heart could dream for. Now you are studying veterinarian medicine, and I'm learning other things. This is so much less than I hoped for. Are we really finished?

"Neill, Neill! My heart feels hollow yet full. Wounds from the surgery of removing you from my life are still tender, I guess. My way of letting go has been to stop all communication with you. Sorry. This is the best I can do right now. My gut flip-flopped when Mom wrote me that you were already dating someone else. I broke up with you because I wasn't ready for marriage, but, I'd hoped that you would wait for me! I'll never forget all the wonderful adventures we had together, cycling San Diego County and swimming in the Pacific. I'm not ready to let go of the feeling that you are *the one*. Maybe I'll never recover from you, my *first love*." I write this letter in my head as I pedal, not planning to send it.

Only one hundred eighteen miles stretch between Yuma and

Gila Bend, Arizona. Pedaling against the blustery, north-west wind, this stretch is taking *forever*. Sand in my eyes and nose, at times I pump my legs but don't gain ground! I tie my red bandana across my nose and mouth, cowboy-style, to minimize the sting on my face and the damage to my lungs and sinuses. Even so, sometimes it blows so hard, it knocks the breath right out of me, reminding me of when I fell twenty feet from a swing set and whacked into a tree before landing on the ground when I was only six years old. You try to inhale but no air comes in. *Ouooooch*!

Grunting like a cave woman, I trudge up, up, up—"The desert is not flat!" I bellow in my brain. On our family trips across country to visit relatives in Baltimore, it appeared to be flat, as I viewed the scenery from the back seat of our big Black Ford. Now, I see and feel hundreds of dips and hills, dips and hills... . Dips are good because I can coast and gain speed as well as have temporary breaks from the relentless wind. Uphill is annoying; I have to put my shoes back on to walk Chariot. I feel irritable, grumpy. Maybe I need to eat a more balanced diet (I eat dates and cactus for breakfast, lunch, and dinner). Perhaps the newness of my adventure is wearing off. Am I depressed? Why am I doing this? God, please remind me.

All of nature is still in hibernation here and I feel like lying down with it until spring comes. The monotony of the winter desert drives me to desperation. Bored to distraction, even road kill becomes entertainment. The stinking, rotting piles of animal debris become bits of art, splattered on a canvas of grey pavement. A portrait of violent death lay in a circle of brown feathers. One large feather sticks straight up out of the center, like a primitive sundial. What kind of bird had it been? Another splotch, a brown patch of fur, lies flat-tened in the perfect silhouette of a coyote, eyeballs pecked clean by preying scavengers. I laugh shamelessly, trying not to breath in sand. Instead, I inhale the putrid scent of death. These critters got much less than they hoped for; but better them than me.

I enter the bustle of traffic in Gila Bend, Arizona. How can there be so many cars in the middle of the desert? This one-street town is the junction of three highways on their way to the two major cities of Phoenix and Tucson. That's why. Tragedy strikes me here. While I travel Highway 84, heading south east to Tucson, a speeding black car bulldozes straight for me. Chariot and I veer off the road just in time to avoid a collision. Visions of road kill flash through my brain as I fly through the air to land in a bush twenty feet from the shoulder.

Tasting the bitter bile of my regurgitated stomach juice, I feel the warm trickle of blood dripping down both my legs. Is this how the animals feel as they lay dying? Looking at my legs, I see dozens of three-pronged burrs protruding from them, stuck in me like thumbtacks. Better than I could have hoped, no skin is missing. No body parts have been filed down by the raspy pavement. I glance up, dazed, to see three horned toads equally stunned, staring with beady, bugged-out eyes, their bodies puffed up to twice their usual size. I landed right in their front yard!

Chariot looks pathetic. His handlebars are twisted; the basketful of my worldly possessions lay strewn about a road-side garden of prickly pear cactus. Worse yet, Chariot's front tire is already completely flat, with dozens of deadly sharp thorns deeply imbedded in its rubber.

"Praise God that I'm still in town." Prayer lightens the dark cloud forming in my mind. I push my injured chariot across the road to a gas station. Blood drips into my *Keds*, staining them a darker color of red. I will go back for my belongings later.

"Hi, Wayne," I say, reading the name embroidered on the shirt of the gas station attendant. He looks a few years younger than me, but his air of maturity and confidence puts me at ease.

"Howdy," he replies. "I saw what happened. That was sure a close one. If I didn't know better, I'd say the driver of that car did that on purpose ... You okay?" Removing his blue cap, he combs his fingers through his short, sandy-blond hair. Mmm ... handsome!

"I think so. Do you have any clean rags and band aids?" I ask, beginning the painful process of removing the burrs from my legs right in the gas station parking lot.

"I have everything you need, including plenty of patches for your bicycle," his riveting blue eyes full of compassion as he speaks. While he removes the front tire to assess the damage, he asks about my trip. When I inform him that I'm cycling across the United States of America to get an education, he chuckles. "I guess you got more than you bargained for today. Did you learn anything from almost getting creamed by a car?" His direct look demands a serious answer.

"I know God is watching out for me. I also feel much safer out in nature than I do in this manmade jungle." Is there any purpose in what happened to me?

We work together and patch thirteen holes in Chariots' tire. The repairs in the tube look like one giant patch. But it holds the air. I retrieve all of my gear and rinse the blood out of my Keds. The rest of the day, I sit in the shade, writing letters, sketching, and talking to Wayne while he pumps gas and wrenches Chariot's handle bars back to true. I accept an invitation to eat dinner with Wayne and a few of his buddies, after he finishes his work.

About five p.m. we hop into his old, red jalopy, and head to his favorite café, a two-story place at the west edge of town. There we meet his three best buddies, Charlie, Brad, and Red—best described as a younger and more dignified version of *The Three Stooges*. I keep this thought to myself, chuckling mysteriously off and on through the evening whenever I think about it.

Wayne buys me burgers, fries, and several pops. I thank him repeatedly, feeling guilty. I have only a few pennies left from my lettuce-packing job. I don't even know where I'm sleeping tonight! We all play the pinball machine, dance to blaring jukebox tunes, and *gab*. What's special about these guys? I couldn't put my finger on it, but they kind of glow, happy to be who they are—content, I guess.

Suddenly, I hear voices shouting from the front of the already noisy, crowded room. A huge man swaggers in the front door, towering above the people who hover around him.

"Oh, my gosh, I think he's *Zorro*," I whisper. Hard to tell without his mask and cape, but ... dark-haired, dark-skinned, muscular, and middle-aged but gorgeous. The man stops every few steps to sign pieces of paper people hastily push toward him. Then he continues to saunter toward the fountain counter.

"He's here," Red says. His teenage freckles glow brighter. "I'm making a phone call to tell the other guys." He runs for the phone booth.

"Who? What's all the excitement about?" I ask Maria, our exotic Spanish waitress.

"I'm going to get his autograph when he comes over here," she says, too overcome to answer my question.

"Here he comes," says Wayne, pointing. "Gee, all the movie stars stop here! Oh, I know who he is. It's John Carroll. I heard he's here to film another western with MGM." As Wayne jumps up from his seat to get a better look, he continues, "He's starring opposite Wild Bill Elliot. I think the western is called *The Fabulous Texan*, or something like that."

I notice Mr. Carroll's grand manner; his arrogant smirk annoys me. I remember some of the movies he starred in. *Zorro Rides Again* is his oldest. His more recent pirate adventures had kept me on the edge of my seat. He always portrays a dashing, gallant, and bold hero who is *masterful* with women. This then is his eminence, in person. I turn to walk away; because, though he looks like a tall, dark, handsome prince—every woman's dream—he also seems too absorbed in his own conceit.

Zorro suddenly changes direction and makes a beeline for me, blocking my path to the jukebox. He swiftly plants his huge body directly in my path and a foot away from my face! "Now, who's this? Don't you want my autograph too?" My mouth gapes but no words come out. There's no doubt he's addressing me. My new friends quickly explain to him, proudly, that my name is Norma Jean Belloff, and that I'm bicycling across the United States. I stare up into Zorro's blue-grey eyes, mesmerized by his powerful presence, in spite of myself. His penetrating gaze softens.

"Norma Jean! Why, my wife and I have a good friend who's real name is Norma Jean. You probably know her as Marilyn Monroe. Both she and my daughter are just a few years older than you," he says leaning closer. Next, Mr. Carroll grabs me with both his hands by the front of my plaid flannel shirt and lifts all one hundred thirty-nine pounds of me straight up off the floor! As I dangle he asks,

"What would you do if some fellow grabbed you like this?" I gasp, still speechless. After a few seconds, he puts me gently back on my feet.

"No one except you has dared to treat me so roughly!" I wiggle to get free, surprised at my own bravado. Then the actor bellows with laughter, like my father would have.

"I bet you'll get there, by Golly! I think you've got the spunk it takes." After a pause, he lowers his voice. "I want to go home to New Orleans for Mardi Gras. I've got shrimp boats to check on too, but MGM says no." Whispering now, for only my ears to hear, he continues, "I'm supposed to have everything, but in reality, you are the one who has it all. I envy you your freedom. Can I have your autograph?"

He seems serious, so, stifling nervous giggles, I ceremoniously sign a napkin and give it to him. In return he quickly tucks a *ten spot* in the upper pocket of my Pendleton. As I try to give it back, he frowns, so I keep it and say,

"Thank you." Handing me a card he says,

"These are friends of mine in El Paso. Call on them for help, if you need it." Then, he wanders away to sit down to order a meal. He's not so bad after all. John Carroll had won me over in less than five minutes. His kindness is more than I'd hoped for in Gila Bend and I feel *lighter than air* as my new friends and I chat quietly until Mr. Carroll leaves the restaurant.

"Would you like to go to our Methodist youth group meeting?" Wayne asks, finally. "I'm the president, and I'll be speaking tonight." This was more than I'd hoped for! It had been a long time since I'd been to a youth group at my Baptist church. When we reach the tiny building where they meet, I automatically sit with the boys. I've always felt more comfortable around boys than girls. The girls here stare at me as they sit in a tidy row on the opposite side of the room from us. The way they stare reminds me of my sister and other girls all through my school years. Is it jealousy? Why would anybody be jealous of me, anyway? Neill used to tell me I'm pretty. But, when I look in the mirror, all I notice are my crooked brows and eyeteeth that stick out like vampire fangs! I smile my sweetest, and stay near the boys.

The new boy, Tommy, sits next to me. Eerie. He could be Buddy's twin; down to the scruffy way he dresses. No one seems to notice that he's what my mother would call a *bum*. My heart goes out to him. During the meeting Wayne shares his testimony of faith and reads a few of his favorite scriptures to inspire us. Now I know why he and his friends seem so different. I feel peace and contentment wash over the room. But they are not for me. I need to help Tommy.

As I leave the church, I take the ten spot that Mr. Carroll donated to my trip and slip it quietly into the hand of the pastor's wife as she stands by the doorway. She winks and smiles. The point of this trip is to be independent and take care of myself, without donations from my family or others. I feel less guilty after giving it away, even though I have only a few cents left to my name.

Next, the entire youth group piles into several cars to go on a joy ride in the desert. After all, what else is there to do in such a tiny town? A tiny bit of moon illuminates the sand and cactus as some of us roar around in Wayne's old-fashioned Ford. Tires slightly deflated to gain better traction in the sand, we twist, turn, and bounce across the desert sand. Like on a rollercoaster, at the Mission Beach Boardwalk back home, we holler and laugh, occasionally choking on the dust and cool air blowing in through the *jalopy's* broken back window.

I sit by Tommy, in the back seat, as we cruise back to town. He stares silently at me and I don't know what to say.

Finally, he blurts out something about wanting to get away from his problems. Announcing that he will hitchhike to Tucson the next day, his face lights up when I tell him I'll look him up when I get there myself. Was this more than he hoped for?

As I lay in my sleeping roll, safely snuggled on a cot next to the cabin of a Highway Police Officer and his family, Sigh! If I'm using this trip to try to get away from my problems, it's certainly backfiring on me. Everywhere I go I meet people who remind me of the loved ones I've left behind!

"God, please use me to help Tommy," I pray. Like Buddy, troubled by things he cannot talk about, I feel miserable thinking about both of them being alone and homeless in a world that could easily use them. This is so much less than what I hope for either of them. God, do I have the right to want it all? Can we use life without abusing it or the people in the world? Or is it as father would say, *dog eat dog*? If even a movie star who I thought had it all doesn't really, then what chance have I? Perhaps I'm expecting too much from life. Is that why I'm disappointed much of the time? But if I put a limit on what I can expect, how will I ever know what can be mine? Who sets the limit on what we get out of life anyway? I'll find some answers to these questions before I finish my trip, right, God?

CHAPTER 6

Angels in New Mexico

February / March 1947

Tucson, Arizona, is a disappointment. I stop at the main post office. No message from Tommy. My heart sinks. I want to see him, a familiar face in a sea of strangers. Besides, God put him in my heart, and once God puts a person in my heart, they never come out. Ill pray for him anyway and always wonder how he is. Be well, Tommy.

Next I look up John Carroll's friends who he suggested could help me. They're kind but offer me no work, suggesting instead that I contact the owner of the Lemmon Mountain Lodge. Lemmon Mountain. I like the sound of that. Perhaps I can work as a waitress there. So disappointed, hungry and tired, I leave Tucson, wiping its dust from my feet and find work and lodgings after a steep ride to the top of Lemmon Mountain; a respite from the monotony of the desert.

Rested and well fed after working eight days at the Lodge, I have a little cash in my pocket again and fond memories of the *fiesta of fun and friends* on top of a mountain. I continue across Arizona, the land of desert, and more desert.

When I die, I want to be an angel; specifically, a guardian angel, powerful and protective. Not that I understand death yet. No one I'm close to has died. Not even in the Big War. My pastor informed me, when I asked him, that people can't be angels. Wretched luck! But why does my Bible say beware of strangers because they might be angels unawares? Do pastors know everything? Unable to reconcile myself to this disappointment, I continue to hope that my pastor is wrong. Sorry, Pastor.

I think Shirley Temple is an angel, and I've always aspired to be like her. However, Mother said that although I can sing and dance as well as Shirley, she wouldn't allow me to be a movie star; I'm already too self-centered. I wonder if Shirley is really as angelic as she appears on the big screen. Only her mother would know for sure; but I still think she's an angel.

Thus rambles my tired brain as I continue cycling east on Highway 80. Only a tiny road sign marks the spot when I cross the state line into New Mexico. This state smells the same as the last two states; grassy, sagey, and clean. However, the terrain is different. A series of small mountains with gentle valleys nestled in between, have replaced the monotony of the Arizona *Badlands*. I stop to fill my canteen and check Chariot's tire pressure in a town named Rodeo, nestled at the foot of the Pello Nulla Mountain range. This place offers no work, so I continue my climb. Up and up, sometimes gradual, sometimes not, until the next golden valley comes into view, framed by another wonderful, uniquely shaped range of mountains. Painted on the horizon in purples, blues, and grays, the jagged towers stand full of mystery and promise.

The next valley looks dryer, and plant life is limited; the locals call it Grease Wood desert. How did the wood get greasy? I coast carefully down the gradual decline, dodging potholes and road critters. Mirages are plentiful here. Something to do with the declination of the sunbeams, but my mind doesn't comprehend them. Magically, time after time, shimmering lakes of water appear in the middle of the road half a mile ahead of me. I say to Chariot, "Boy, that water looks good," only to be disappointed when I arrive at the spot to discover that the water has magically dried up!

Slightly ahead on my left, in the midst of a valley full of shimmering bronze grass, there appears a huge lake. Convinced this time it is real, I say, "What a great place to go for a swim and get cleaned up." I sniff my underarms and grimace. But when I stop at the side of the road to check my map, there is no lake there!

Disappointed again, I push on and up the next gradual incline. At the crest of this *Valley of Fools*, road signs warn, *Strong winds possible, with zero visibility due to shifting sand.* Not just possible, but inevitable I discover too late. Instead of a refreshing swim in water, Chariot and I swim through a sand storm, crawling at a snail's pace. My patience is worn thin; a hearty meal long overdue, I hope the next town will provide me with food, rest, and work.

Then a voice whispers, "There is no God."

"What?" I yell at the wall of flying sand around me. "If there's no God, then who are you?" I challenge.

"Your mind," the voice replies. Oh, that's just great! My pastor wisely warned me that most people go through times of doubt about the existence of God. But this is very inconvenient! "Why do I have to go through this right now?" I whine, barely moving my lips to keep sand from slipping in and grinding the enamel off my teeth.

I try to think about other things but the voice keeps coming back. Spying a turn-out a few feet ahead, I pull Chariot to a squeaky stop. Still straddling my bike, I close my eyes and talk to my mind; the wall of sand protecting me from possible disconcerting stares of fellow travelers, though I haven't seen a human being for hours. Motionless, eyes squeezed closed, I allow the *goo* in my mind to slide down the side of the mountain where there is no God like the one I'd learned to believe in.

No God, no conscience ... no conscience, no guilt ... I like the *yellow brick road* of my thinking so far! I continue. No creator, no creation ... no creation, no love. Uh oh. Did I take a wrong turn somewhere? I simply can't imagine a world without God's unchanging love. Unable to continue down this avenue of thinking right now, I *put a cork in the goo*, swing my feet to the pedals, and grunt forward into the white oblivion of the storm.

Too stormy to sleep outside, I forge ahead through the dusk and dust until I reach Lordsburg. This town, sprawling across the next valley, surely would offer me money, water, and rest. I pedal eagerly down the highway now, the Big Burro Mountain Range towering to the northeast and the aptly named Pyramid mountains directly to the south, protecting the town and me from the horrible wind.

"Excuse me, sir, excuse me!' I scream out desperately when I come within voice range of a shepherd riding the range near the road, straddling his dusty horse. "Do you know where I can get some work in exchange for something to eat?" I hope I don't sound as desperate as I feel.

"There ain't no work I can think of, but why don't you settle down at my place for the night. I got plenty of vitals and a cot to sleep on," he offers. The first real cowboy I ever talked to, a *scruffy angel*, he welcomes me into his one-room home, perfumed with the pungent smell of horses, leather, and sheep. What a prairie palace it seems to me, compared to the sand-blown desert floor that has been my bed the last few days. I feel no fear for my safety. After all, if a horse could trust a cowboy, why couldn't I? Perhaps viewing too many western movies had created my delusion, but I have to trust him, trust God, if He exists, for protection.

Well rested and still safe the next day, I enjoy a cowboy breakfast cooked for me by my lank and bristled hero. Bacon, sausage, egg and huge slabs of buttered bread; it's enough food to fuel me for the whole day. With hair and clothes still full of sand, I promise to write him and let him know how I fare. I pump uphill against the wind once more, hoping a letter from home will be waiting for me in El Paso, Texas. My desperate situation is temporary. But what if I had no family to help me out? I shudder to think of it.

Bubbling over with gratitude for a full stomach, I sing, "Home, Home on the Range" to the prairie dogs, collared lizards, and road runners. Then, gradually climbing southeast into another low row of hills, I discover the *Continental Divide*. Somewhere between the tiny towns of Separ and Gage stands a modest wooden sign stating the elevation— four thousand five hundred eighty-five feet. I'm shocked! How could I have climbed up so high since sea level back in Arizona?

I wish I could test out the theory that all rivers to the east of this spot flow east and all rivers to the west flow west. However, just as water has to flow one way or the other, I realize I would not last long with a divided mind about God. Some people call it *riding the fence*. I feel wobbly; out of balance. *A mind divided against itself cannot stand.* Eventually, the *goo* in my mind would have to choose a course; God or no God; that is the question. I sniff the air, seeking scientific evidence with my five senses, something tangible that would help me choose God. Gradually, terror worms its way into my heart. What is happening to me? How can I be thinking like this?

Pedaling and pondering, an oasis of civilization comes into view in the center of this high desert valley. Bowlin's trading post, a train station, a church, and a few houses stand, clustered like a wagon train in the middle of a prairie. Stopping to rest, I marvel at the ancient trading post, built log-cabin style. The musk of old animal hides tickles my nose as I enter. A *welcome sign* boasts that the store had been there since the eighteen-hundreds. I believe it!

I fill my canteen with fresh water, then, having no money to spend, I browse, admiring the fascinating array of trinkets and staple supplies displayed on slab shelves. Alone except for the clerk behind the counter, several minutes pass before he speaks to me. "Would ya like to try a delicacy of the area?" he asks, then, he drops something small into his mouth. Chuckling, he holds out a small box that contains dried brown worms; fat, round, and about one inch long. I shrug and pick one out, crunching it between my teeth. Not much flavor. My stomach grumbles appreciation for a welcome though unusual meal as I take a few more. "Thank you," I mumble as I chomp. The clerk just nods and eats a few more himself.

Suddenly, I blurt out, "Do you believe in God?" I look around to make sure it was me who had asked him that. Mother always said it was rude to ask strangers personal questions and, that rudeness is a sign of weak character. I hope this isn't true of me.

"Well, I think everybody does, young lady, whether they like to admit it or not," he replies, matter-of-factly. "Otherwise, they'd surely lose their marbles." He taps his left temple with his weathered pointer finger for emphasis. "See that little church just up the street? That's the one

I attend," he continues, pointing through the window, to the weather-beaten white church, not much wider than its welcoming front doors. On the top sits an oversized steeple, like a giant finger pointing straight at heaven. Then, the kind old clerk winks, pats me gently on the shoulder, and goes about his business. I stand there some minutes in his store, chewing on worm crumbs, digesting what he'd just told me, and eyeballing the dusty wood plank floors under my feet to see if any of my marbles were rolling there.

After thanking the clerk for his generosity, I re-mount Chariot. Something is not right. I dismount to check Chariot's tires. The rear tire is flat! How could this happen when I don't remember running over anything sharp? Drat! I haven't replaced my bicycle pump since it was stolen. Instead, I've relied on gas stations along the way to supply me with one when I needed it.

I stand next to my bicycle, brow furrowed in frustration. What should I do? At this moment, a motorcycle slides into the parking area, stirring up a big puff of sandy dust. The young rider hops off his bike and nods, then enters the trading post. I stand in the same spot, still pondering my dilemma, as he saunters back out, soda pop in hand, a friendly smile on his face. He's not much older than me and dashingly handsome in his brown leather motorcycle gear.

"What's wrong? You look all bent out of shape," he asks.

Unaware my darkened mood is so obvious, "I've got a flat, and no way to fix it."

"Well, I've come all the way from Pensacola, Florida, and this is your lucky day! I have a tire pump that will fix you right up!" I am instantly infected by his cheerful attitude. As he proceeds to help me fix the flat, he continues, "My sister and I work in a motorcycle shop in Pensacola.

You ought to stop in and see us if you make it that far east." If! Did he doubt I'd make it to my destination?

Carefully jotting down his sister's name, address, and phone number, he hands it to me. I can't believe it. His sister's name is *Angel*! I've never known an Angel before!

"Thank you," is all I can say as I tuck the paper into my little black diary, hoping I would get a chance to meet her.

"You know the secret to my happiness?" His face beams as he looks me straight in the eye. "There's only three things I need. Someone to love, something important to do, and something to look forward to." With that, like *Prince Charming* at the ball, he bows and says, "I've got them all. How 'bout you?" Surprised, I think, then point to my Bible perched in the basket of my bike, which I hadn't read for three days.

"For me, where there's hope, there's happiness. Thank you for reminding me." I remember my favorite Shirley Temple movie, *The Blue Bird*, in which Mytyl learns she can choose to be happy by seeing the good in what she already has. Then Dorothy, in the *Wizard of Oz*, who realizes in the end that contentment can be found in her own back yard.

He smiles even wider, winks, nods, and jumps on his beast to drive gallantly toward the west, disappearing in his trail of dust and smoke. Looking down, I notice that the tire pump still lay on the ground near my bicycle. Oh, no! But he's already just a brown speck on the *black top* far away. I pick up the pump, place it on top of my sleeping roll, and wonder. Is this a careless mistake he made? Is this a random act of kindness? Or is he an *angel*? Sufficient evidence has been presented for now, and the *goo* in my mind flows slowly down the side of the hill that leads me back to faith in God.

The San Andres Mountain Range looms like a massive castle fortress above Las Cruces, the largest city I visit since entering New Mexico. I would surely find work here! I sleep in a farmer's hay pile, soft and warm, and *borrow* chicken eggs, swallowing the slimy insides raw. I leave at dawn, driven by hunger to pursue work in town.

Las Cruces lay lush and green, a prosperous-looking town, most likely watered by the Rio Grande River, which flows southeast on its way to the Gulf of Mexico. I ask for work at fifteen different businesses here, yet the answer is always no. I can't believe it! By evening, clouds block the mild spring sun and the air temperature plummets. Disheartened and very hungry, again, I pedal on southeast. In Mesquite, a tiny town a few miles away, I knock on a farmer's door to ask for a place to sleep. The blonde-haired farmer's wife says no and closes the door, leaving me standing in the rain. At the next ranch, I knock again, panic and desperation setting in. A kindly man—middle aged, olive-skinned with a bushy, black mustache and compassionate brown eyes—welcomes me and gives me food and a cot on his porch.

Kneeling to pray, "Thank you, Lord, for your mercy to me," I whisper before I pass out, lulled to sleep by the soft *mooing* of his cattle. Early the next day the generous farmer allows me to help clean his stockyard. I try to express my gratitude in Spanish and the farmer's eyes mist while he tightly clutches the large wooden crucifix hanging from a leather strap around his neck.

"I am the one who thanks you, my dear," the farmer speaks in perfect English. Why? For treating his family with respect? After eating a hearty dinner of salty beans, rice, and homemade tamales with his family, strength and hope return. Eager to get to El Paso, Texas, before nightfall, I say goodbye to the farmer and to a state full of savage beauty ... and angels.

Chapter 7
Texas Gold

February / March 1947

El Paso or bust. I climb the last steep and winding slope of Highway 80 that passes through the gap in the Organ Mountain Range. The land stretches for miles polka dotted with dormant mesquite bushes, ocotillo, and prickly pear cacti. Long-horned cattle graze along either side of the road. I'm not sure what they're eating, the ground looks barren to me. I still follow the railroad tracks and the majestic Rio Grande. How can water be flowing uphill? The illusion is convincing.

I think of John Carroll's new movie, *The Fabulous Texan,* as I labor up the long, steep incline. I wonder if I'll meet anyone *fabulous* in Texas. All I know is that I'll make a beeline for downtown and the YWCA, where showers and real beds wait. The post office could wait until first thing tomorrow morning to get news from *home, sweet home.* Then I vow to find a *real* job.

I climb one last hill as the sun takes a peek at the world from behind huge storm clouds before retiring for the night. Magically, a glittering, golden city appears perched on the hillside to my right as I reach the top. Lit up by the retiring sunbeams, the flat-topped houses appear to be stacked, like stairs, up the side of the steep hill. Painted a rainbow of pastel colors, it reminds me of Tijuana, Mexico, back home.

The Rio Grande winds large and lazy below me, flowing between me and this city on the hill. Is this Ciudad Juarez, Mexico?

Straight ahead of me, on the left side of the Rio, sprawls another city, with towering buildings and splendid colonial-style homes step-stoning up the hillside. Just a bit farther, the rest of the city comes into view, nestled in the longest, broadest valley I've viewed on this trip so far. Hemmed in on the right by an endless mountain range heading east and west, the whole valley luxuriates with lush, green trees and farm fields as far as my tired eyes can see. Jeepers! Everything *is* bigger in Texas. This *Lone Star State* bursts with wealth, variety, and grandeur so big that people once thought it was a separate country.

The March air is cold; a storm is brewing. Thank you, God, for perfect timing. I pedal with purpose toward the downtown towers built of red and tan brick; many doorways here are adorned with massive but graceful colonial-style pillars and stairways. Streetlights already glowing, there is still bustling activity everywhere. People move about in cars, busses, and on horseback. The commotion is confusing after so many days of solitude and open space in New Mexico. I find the YWCA after dark; the wind blows fiercely and rain pelts down as I enter the well-lit building.

"I'd like to spend a few days here, please," I tell the young clerk at the front desk.

"Sure you can," she says, smiling. "You can share a room for fifty cents per night." Now comes the hard part.

"Well, you see," I stammer, "I'm completely out of cash at the moment." I glance up at her with pleading, tired eyes. "Tomorrow I plan to look for work; then I can pay you," I continue, wondering what my fate will be.

Unconcerned, "Wait here a moment," she says with

a wonderful Texan drawl. I like Texas already. I thaw out quickly as I stand in the heated lobby, staring at the ornate mosaics adorned with gold inlay that decorate the ceiling and walls. The clerk returns in less than a minute.

"There are some girls here that are willing to let you bunk with them. They say they'll pay your way." She motions for me to leave my bike in the lobby and follow her to my new lodgings.

"Thank you," is all I can say. Texans' hearts are as big as their state. What would I have done if I could not have stayed here? I shiver, not wanting to think any more about that now.

February 26

My newfound hope turns to despair this morning. No mail waits for me at the El Paso post office. I hope Neill might finally try to contact me. I had heard nothing from him since I started this trip. Although I'd broken off the engagement last autumn, saying that I needed more *salad days* before I was ready for marriage, I thought that *true love waits*. Neill has nestled himself deep inside my heart and life and I don't want to let go completely. Perhaps this is selfish and unrealistic. "God, what do you have to say about it?" I pray.

Violating my newfound sense of freedom, I wire a request for money from Mom and Pop. Immediately, they wire me twenty dollars, no questions asked. They know that if I'm desperate enough to ask, I'm near starvation. *Out of touch* with home since Arizona, my parents are, apparently, glad to hear from me.

February 27

Today, a package arrives from Pop. He has never given me

a present in my life! I hastily unwrap the small box. An ornately decorated, expensive-looking gold watch and band greets me, along with a simple note stating "Happy Birthday, from your father." I'd forgotten that my twentieth birthday is only a few days away!

Father does have a love of beautiful things! Quite sure that he had picked this gift out himself, I ceremoniously place it on my wrist with as much pomp as a queen during coronation. Gee, how it sparkles! Pop knows that I don't care about time and schedules, especially not on this trip. What is he trying to tell me? This gift must be a symbol of his love and care for me, and I cherish it, however out of character it is for him to send it. Perhaps it is true what they say, that absence makes the heart grow fonder. Crazy, but I like it!

March 5

Six days of *pounding the pavement* for work and I'm still jobless. Part of the problem is that Mexico sits just across the Rio Grande, accessible by footbridge at the south end of downtown El Paso. Merchants tell me that Mexican labor is cheaper and easier to boss.

March 6

Eureka! I pose, wearing only shorts and a swim suit top, modeling for an art class at the local college. Twenty-five dollars! Not bad pay for one-half day of *lolling* about in a warm room with a cluster of friendly students. I'm not going to pay Mom and Pop back yet, though. I need this money to get me out of town and down the road a-ways. I promise myself to pay them back when I get a *tad* more ahead, financially.

March 8

I meet a cowboy named Steve. Like a younger Gary Cooper in *Along Came Jones*, he comes complete with long legs; a shy, gentle spirit; and a love of singing. Quite a captivating, country gentleman, he moves in rhythm to his fluid Texan drawl. Are all Texas men like this? He invites me to see the bull and cockfights in Ciudad Juarez, the town just across the Rio Grande. I agree to go out of curiosity and a desire to dull the ache in my heart for Neill.

The plan works. Delightfully romantic. However, the cock and bull fights upset me. Steve holds me back, more than once, from jumping into the ring to save the poor animals from their certain deaths. We leave before the end of either show. Wandering through the streets full of peddlers and shops, we devour candied yam and tacos while slurping tangy tamarind juice. At the end of the day I say *adios* with a promise to write. Like the surveyor I'd met in El Centro, Steve is sweet but not for me. Am I being heartless? Youth can be an excuse for many poor decisions, and I won't be twenty for four more days. Though good looks, charm, and money are certainly appealing, I know I need more in a mate, to be content. God, I promise to look for answers to my many questions in Your *Word*.

March 9

Snow descends on El Paso! A rare event in this area. I realize I will be pedaling in this weather tomorrow. How will Chariot perform?

March 10

The snow melts and the rain stops. I pay my debts at the YWCA in El Paso and say goodbye to the *cherubs* who had taken me in and *mothered* me. God, I begin to see why I need other human beings in my life. Their kindnesses are like hugs from you, with skin on. I want to be like you, with skin on too. Amen.

Chapter 8
Here and Now in Texas

March 1947

The air temperature is a brisk fifty degrees as I cycle east and then north on Highway 62, heading for the famous Carlsbad Caverns. They're dubbed the "largest natural hole ever discovered in this earth" in the National Parks Brochure. My curiosity drives me on in spite of cold weather and the windy, steep climb through more desert mountains. Chariot maneuvers well on icy, snowy roads and by midmorning, El Paso sinks into its mountain cup behind me. Goodbye El Paso.

I smell like a wet sheep, but I'm warm. Packing three layers of shirts under my newly washed Pendleton, a pair of wool gloves and a knit wool hat, I stop every few miles and pull off the cap to relieve the itching and scratch my head.

Mom says I'm a dreamer, and, that while my mind yearns for the future, I often miss what is good about the *here and now*. "Be more practical," she would scold at least once a week. In her last letter she wrote, "Keep a nest egg to fall back on, so you won't get so hungry again." Mother, you would be proud of how wisely I spend my money now. I'm sure I have enough to last me until I reach San Antonio.

Chariot and I cross twenty miles of desert and then begin the climb up five miles of mountains, the Huecos. The natural beauty around me takes my breath away, a *wonderland* of colors and shapes. Orange sand flows gracefully down the side of Hueco foothills, just as the molten slag had flowed down the pile of waste at the *smelter plant* I toured in El Paso. In places, the slopes look as though they are man-laid masonry—square stone on square stone, forming long grey/brown marbled walls along the edge of the road.

Other curving hills bring back a memory nearly forgotten; a pineapple plantation in Hawaii. The pineapple plants here are really wide-spaced yuccas, just beginning to bloom. From my childhood eyes I can almost see a Hawaiian worker in the hillside field. As I ride on, a flood of memories come—the bland, creamy taste of fresh ground poi, raw sugar cane; the smell of the sea mixed with tropical flowers; the feel of my bare feet in the sand while running wild with a pack of brown-skinned, half naked playmates; the rustle of our grass hula skirts as we dance in school; and all the colors of nature painted on the Tapa cloths that hang on the walls of our family home.

Several hours later, I find myself on a platter-shaped plateau. I laugh at a rosy rock mountain crest, peeking over the plateau's edge on my left like a curious giant, standing on tiptoe to see me. This must be Guadalupe Peak, the highest point in Texas at an elevation of almost nine thousand feet, they say.

Thousands of acres of cattle range fill this western corner of the state. Now, in my mind, the yucca become cattle. "Hello," I holler. But, instead of bolting away as steer often do, the Yucca hold their poses and only slightly rustle their dark green, dagger-tipped blades in response. Slanting sunbeams gleaming on the lolling highway remind me of the saying that *the streets of heaven are paved with gold*. The streets of *my* heaven are glistening silver; the pebble masses stuck in the tar of the road, catch light on their polished sides and glitter like a pathway of gems. I look up and twist Chariot's handle bars just in time to miss an *auto-comet* beeping a warning as it passes, heading the opposite direction. Whew! Close one, God … Automatically, my knees rise and fall. The comet vanishes over a golden swell. I smile dreamily.

Leaving this glitter-grassed plain, I enter another, another, and still another until I lose count. Would I be eternally moving in this calm? As if in answer to my thought, the next swell bows to my muscle power and reveals sixty more miles of Texas sprawling before me. I pump over the Huecos without walking once.

I hope to discover why Texans are so proud. At dusk, the *town* I'd been anticipating finally arrives. Consisting of an auto-repair garage, a house, and a café, it stands like a pioneer outpost for settlers who traveled here long ago. I chuckle as I warm my hands by the roaring wood stove in one corner of the family-run café. Quite different from the *town* of San Diego.

"I brought my own dinner, but I'd like to fill my canteen if I could, please," I request of the homespun young woman who stands behind the counter. She casually holds an infant slung on her right hip while holding a cup of coffee in the other hand.

"Sure, honey. But, what're you doing out all by yourself on a cold day like this?' she asks. "Don't you want a cup of hot chocolate to warm your bones?' There's that wonderful

Texan drawl again, as big and wide as the country surrounding us.

No more said, the family *takes me in*. We eat dinner, the two parents, their young child, and the grandma; they offer me a bed in a small cabin behind the café. In exchange, I answer their many questions about what I'm doing and why. I offer to wash the dishes, grateful to stay warm a little longer, then I sink into unconsciousness, cocooned in my snug sleeping roll, safe in the cabin, pitch-black silence around me.

The next morning they feed me a huge country breakfast. Juicy steak, fresh eggs, buttery biscuits, and cream-topped milk. My stomach full to the point of bursting, I brave to ask them, "What is it that you like best about living in Texas?"

"The friendly people," the mother and father answer in unison, then look at each other and laugh.

Still curious, I ask, "What is it about Texas that makes people so friendly?"

'It's the wonderful weather. The sun shines more often than not," the father offers.

The grandmother adds, "Because there's so much room for everyone that no one feels crowded, and yer grateful when you finally see another human being."

The young mother continues, "No neighbors to crowd you, and when you take a breath, it's got a clean taste to it ... like no one's ever used it before."

Again, the young father speaks up, "We like room to stretch, and where you step, it seems like no foot's been set there before."

This whole family speaks in *poetry of loving kindness*, reminding me of an old Chinese proverb I read once. *One kind word can warm three winter months*. Spoken words are actions, aren't they? They have the power to chill or to warm, to hurt or to heal. I pray silently, from memory, Psalm 19:14. "May the words of my mouth and the meditation of my heart be acceptable in your sight, Oh Lord, my rock and my redeemer." The warmth of this family's words will stay with me forever. I wave goodbye and pedal off again, determined to make White City before the day ends.

I arrive, early evening, in White City, New Mexico, the home of the world-famous Carlsbad Caverns National Park. The locals say that tourists come from all over the world, even in the middle of winter! There are no accommodations for overnight sleepers in the National Park, so I stay at a hotel in White City; the cheapest room costs one dollar and fifty cents per night. I pay in advance for two nights.

Early the next morning, drawn to the *wonder of nature* as if by a magnet, I pedal to the entrance of the cave. The brochure says a tour of the caverns takes five hours on foot. There's electricity and even elevators down to the seven hundred fifty foot level, and lunch is available at the bottom. Entrance fee, one dollar and fifty cents. Always cool and humid below, tourists are not allowed to wander alone there.

At the entrance, the cave looms formidable, like a colossal gaping mouth, and I hesitate before I decide to go in with the other fifty people who dare enter with me. As I wind down the zigzag cement path into the cavernous mouth, I cringe, shivering, claustrophobic. Is this how Jonah felt as he entered the whale's mouth? Other thoughts creep in. What if the ceiling collapses? What if the electricity goes out? What if I get lost in the twenty-three miles of tunnels in the dark? Then a grim memory from long ago surfaces;

a flash of being very small and locked in a closet under a staircase. I remember staying there so long that I peed my pants. Had I been naughty and was being punished, or was it an accident that I'd been incarcerated for hours? Who would put me there, so vulnerable? Perhaps it was a dream. But what dream could evoke such terror?

I keep walking, herded along by the throng of tourists behind me. Who would have thought I would feel this way about a silly cave? I silently beg God to relieve me of the panic that rises in my throat. I don't want to scream! The sound would echo off the walls of the hundreds of chambers below ground. Perhaps it would echo all the way to hell; sometimes I wonder if I deserve to go there. Suddenly, I feel blue and morose, but it's too late to turn back now.

Inside the cave, I view the first room full of stalagmites and stalactites lit up like Christmas trees. I close my eyes. "Norma, stay in the here and now," a voice says, clear as day. "Don't let fear keep you from realizing your dreams." Allowing the warmth of the voice to wash over my body, I feel cleansed and at peace.

In the here and now, the guide describes the discovery of the caves. The story goes that Jim White was herding cattle when he saw a dark, moving column rising out of the ground. He investigated and found a natural opening in the earth that led down to the caverns. The dark, smoke- like column proved alive; a moving stream of thousands of bats emerging from the darkness of the caves. White, along with a young Mexican boy, made extensive exploration of the caves, using only a torch, chalk, and string to find their way back. Weren't they both afraid? Did they hear a voice in the cave that calmed them also?

I hadn't planned to bike all the way here to White City. I was going to take a short cut to a small town called Angeles, then continue back south on Highway 285. However, all things in life happen for a reason, don't they? There really is no coincidence, is there? I trust this side trip is meant to be and that what happened in the cave is a gift. There is a right time for everything, and this has been just right. Perhaps I'll understand more when I'm older.

This morning, another surprise! Local park rangers find me at my hotel and deliver a notice for a registered letter to be picked up at the post office. How had Mom known I would be here? I tremble as I hold two letters in my hand. One is from Neill. I would save that for later. Tearing open the one from Mom, I find a ten-dollar bill and a *Happy Birthday* note. Mom has news. Buddy has been found again and is *incarcerated* at Anthony's, a correctional facility for wayward boys. He would stay there a few months. She ends the letter, "You aren't a teenager any more, Love, Mom."

Poor Buddy! He hates confinement more than I do ... at least he is safe. What did he do wrong? Mom left the sordid details out. If he had come with me on this trip, he would be okay now. I could protect him. Buddy, Buddy... . I sob, right there in the post office. Tears fall as I grieve for what I could not do to help him—on my twentieth birthday. *Here and now*, we are far apart, and all I can do is pray for him. Dear God, let your voice come to him to calm his fears also.

Coming out of Carlsbad, I tie on my red bandana for protection from the sun. I'd left my favorite cap hanging on a nail in the hotel at White City. Darn it! I cross swell after swell of creosote bush desert and watch a smiling sunset. I sing to myself to keep happy and accept the colors in the sky as a salute to my birth. But, when I sing "Happy Birthday to me," I have to gulp hard to finish the song.

As dark encroaches, an ominous hand creeps over the range I traverse until it catches and envelopes me. The black, damp, cold windstorm blots everything from my sight. It seems I'm lost forever, fighting the powerful gusts to stay on the road. Darkness arrives. Huge bolts of lightening, followed by deafening thunder increase my terror. Chariot is metal, after all. Doesn't that make me an easy target?

To calm my fear long ago, Mom told me to imagine that thunder came from *little men in the sky, knocking down bowling pins.* Now, visions of hideous giants with mouths as big as the entrance to the Carlsbad Caverns come, throwing deadly bolts at me. I'm ashamed of myself for many things. I fear I'll never be good enough. I fear that I'll disappoint everyone who cares about me. I feel very sorry for myself, *to boot.*

I close out the storm with thoughts of home and memories of Neill's love. Night falls. Settling Chariot into a culvert under the road, in case it rains, I spread my roll among the small, round rocks that lay on the highway's edge. The wind whips at my tarp, which lay over me, anchored by rocks. Flap, flap ...

Then, uninvited, visions of Brown Recluse spiders come to me. Some one warned me that recluse hide under rocks and come out at night. Perfect desert monsters, recluses are able to live without food or water for long periods. Brown, with violin-shaped marks on their backs, they stare with six eyes, arranged in three groups of two, and their bites leave cavernous holes in human flesh. Great! What a bedtime story, and on my birthday, no less.

During the night, a recurring nightmare visits me. In it I open a door, step out into thin air, and fall for eternity, until

I wake. Waking this time, I'm damp and chilled, having slid out from under the poncho and rolled down the embankment while I dreamed. The Northerner isn't blowing any more, but, I'm a lump of ice, so I pack Chariot and moan all the way to the next town, Orla.

Thank God the café is open, even though it's still dark. I thaw out with bacon, eggs, and milk for seventy-five cents. I don't want to leave the cafe because snow is predicted, and I have to cross *such a lot of nothing* before I get to Pecos! So, in the bright light of the warm café, I finally read the letter from Neill. I'd been afraid to read it, expecting rejection. In it he is polite but emotionally distant, providing lots of details about his college days at Stanford University. Though he doesn't promise to wait for me, at least he hasn't forgotten me; that's something.

As if by a miracle, the blue mood lifts from my heart this morning. Psalm 30:5 "Weeping may last for the night, but a shout of joy comes in the morning." The sun is out, the air is still. Glorious! Today, I'll *stop and smell the roses.*

> *Dear Mom:*
>
> *I had no idea that my birthday could be so important to me. Actually, I admit that a very large part of me does not want to grow up. It hit me hard in your last letter when you suggested that it might be a good idea to just skip my birthday and keep on being nineteen. There is something so final about becoming twenty. As you reminded me, I am no longer a teenager.*
>
> *You must be saying your prayers because I'm happy again. That darn lonesome streak passed as*

I pedaled into Alpine, Texas. The sun is out again, and all seems right. I'm thinking about Buddy, imprisoned at "Anthony's." Where will they send him next? Camp Woodson? If they locked me up, I think I would die. I'm addicted to wide-open spaces. I've been singing that ditty you taught me: "Give me land, lots of land under starry skies above, don't fence me in ... ," you know the one. There aren't many fences in Texas so far, and I'm glad.

Thanks for having me, Mom! Can you remember the time when I was fourteen and I wished I hadn't been born? In the "here and now," I've a feeling I will never wish it again. Life is a privilege, isn't it? I can't get over my blessing of have you for a mother. God gave me a head start on everyone for happiness ever after.

Love,
Your daughter, Norma

Chapter 9
Resurrected in Texas

March 1947

At Balmorhea State Park where I spent the night, I wake surrounded by spring and intoxicating earth smells. At the mountain town of Alpine near by, friendly people greet me, astonished that I travel by bicycle during this rainy season. As I devour breakfast, the waitress says, "Weather will improve as you continue south." How encouraging she is!

My internal storm passed during the night also. Today I'm bursting with ambition and love of life, as usual. I'm relieved to realize life does not end at twenty! I feel resurrected, like the tiny fern that grows here. I'm told the fern looks dead most of the year, but when watered by the spring rain, it comes to life and blooms within twelve hours, then continues to flourish for months. Today the world is my oyster again, and I won't give up the search for a pearl.

So begins the long downhill coast south toward the border town of Del Rio. With only five dollars in my pocket, I promise myself to look for work soon. Contrary to my teenage naivety, I realize I can't live on *thin air*. Cactus and water, which I thought were like *manna from heaven* in the Old Testament days, are not enough to fuel my hard-working body. That experiment had failed. Drat!

I stop often to soak in the breathtaking tints of the wildflowers; some delicate and pale, others brilliant and deep, they blend, harmonize, and contrast. The blossom designs thrill me, grace and symmetry in quantities of patterns, set off by equally varying foliage forms. A purple nosegay in green lace; a triumphant arrangement of a scarlet and white waxen cluster surrounded by bristling, dark green swords; and fragile, pale-green cups bob above leaves that lay flat, clinging to the earth. A pink cloud billows, a budding bush on the roadside makes me marvel that these lovely creations can suck their glory from gritty, white particles of soil. Thank you, God, that the world looks lovely again. May it never seem as bleak as it did on my twentieth birthday.

My Poem about Spring

Three days, three nights
The rain fell soft
Upon the earth's hard crust.
Stirred land to life
As love might wrest
An old maid from her rust.
Within a bosom
Fertility wrought.
To dust-dreary eyes
New beauty brought.

East of Sanderson I stop at a sheep ranch owned by the Hs, to ask for work. The husband and wife team put me to work. I assist Mr. H. in herding sheep, and marking lambs, cutting off their tails, and clipping their cute little ears. It's bloody, sticky work. I sleep on their porch after Mrs. H. warns me of mountain lion cubs, honing their hunting skills by slitting the throats of up to sixty of their lambs each night. I marvel that these people don't resent the mountain lions' behavior. They simply say, "After all, the mountain lions were here first." I doubt I would be as calm if my livelihood were threatened.

On my third day with them, I attend church, wearing a tent-like, over-starched Sunday dress loaned to me by Mrs. H. After a huge Sunday dinner, these generous people fill Chariot's basket to overflowing with homemade bread, butter, cheese, and wild honey. This morning, I depart my usual way, waving and promising to write.

As I follow the railroad tracks that run parallel to the highway, I cross the Pecos and Del Rio Rivers and spy my first cardinal. Brilliant red—my favorite color. He looks like an Ocotillo blossom, a tongue of flame on the branch where he sings. Lavender Mountain Laurel perfumes my way. Cactus blooms of Scarlet Hedgehop flowers peek up at me from below the shoulder of the road, and I climb down a cliff to touch them. While there, I see five Mexican men duck into a culvert, carrying gunnysacks over their shoulders. Are they stealing wool, or perhaps trying to sneak across the border? I pretend not to notice. I can't hold it against them to try for a better life. Some illegal behavior can be justified. Little brother Buddy, I hope you are surviving your captivity.

Every time Buddy runs away, he heads for Mexico. What did Buddy find in Mexico that he couldn't find at home? Curiosity renders me fearless, and when I arrive in Del Rio, Chariot's tires turn right and take me straight to Villa Kuna, a Mexican border town a few miles away. As I pedal across the border, patrolled without a gate, I resolve to spend the night with a Mexican family. What would it be like to spend the night in a foreign country and in a home where only Spanish is spoken?

A middle-aged Mexican man driving a beat-up truck stops and offers a ride, as I pedal casually along the dirt road. His grin is too wide. I say "No, thank you," shaking my head. Close by, two women walk, wearing festive dresses and balancing huge baskets of laundry on their heads. I smile and wave, then pull up next to them and stop.

"Could I please spend the night at your house?" I ask, wearing a hopeful smile. They have no clue what I'm saying. I speak *English*; they speak *Spanish*. A flurry of hand signs and arm waving ensues, and, in the end, they gesture me to follow them. That was easy! My curiosity will soon be satisfied.

We sit on blankets or wood stumps, in their one-room hut. A patchwork of cardboard, wood, and tin, it stands the size of our garden shed, back home. I smile, mute, and watch, documenting everything in my heart. The dirt floor is swept smooth. A plaster crucifix hangs on a nail above a red candle, which burns brightly on a shelf next to the door. Posters of bullfights and cigarette ads paper the walls. Oversized red and blue paper flowers bloom out of a clay pot in one corner. The rest of their possessions are stuffed in the baskets and wooden crates that support the flimsy walls of their small home.

Both women pound out corn tortillas after building a fire under the stone grill, located in the center of the room. They chatter and laugh, glancing shyly in my direction. A cluster of scantily clad children surround me, touching my blonde curls, and take turns sitting on Chariot, leaning against a wall, inside their house. This family's language flows graceful and warm, wrapping around me like a colorful serape. The smells in their home are intoxicating. Spices, sweat, wool, and earth. Their simple, generous hospitality lulls me to contentment; I'm not even required to provide witty conversation. Buddy, now I understand why you choose to run here. You feel safe. You can be yourself. There are no big expectations; no pressure to be anything you're not. Smart boy, Buddy.

I spend a restless night sleeping in the same room with seven snoring bodies and dozens of biting chiggers. Today, the young woman, Ophelia, makes it clear that she wants to return to Del Rio with me. When we arrive at the border, the immigration officer stops her. She watches me leave with sad brown eyes; a prisoner in her own country. "Sorry I can't help you as you and your family helped me," I want to tell her, but can't.

Back in Del Rio, I purchase my favorite Mexican candies; white globs of sugar-saturated coconut and creamy brown-sugar patties. I mail them to my family. I send my father a prickly pear cactus. I don't know why; he doesn't like plants, unless it's something he can bake in a pie. I write to him explaining the cactus is an early Easter present. Prickly pears are good to eat once the toughness of the outside is removed. Maybe he's like the prickly pear, all tough and stubbly on the outside.

Will I ever *get the hang* of being a good daughter? I still wear the watch he gave me every day to remind me that he thought about me in a pleasant way. I only wish things were not so awkward between us. Is it this way with all fathers and their daughters, or is there something wrong with my family? I want so much to understand.

After writing all morning in the public library in Del Rio, I wander along, pushing Chariot, hoping to find some work. I approach a fair-skinned lady wearing an apron, grey hair rolled in a tight bun, vigorously weeding her garden.

"Can I please help you weed your garden in exchange for a meal?"

Looking up briefly, "Yes, of course, darlin," is all she says, a sweet smile on her careworn face. She is widowed and lives alone. After a supper of spicy lamb, rice, and greens, we walk to the movies, her treat.

Angel on My Shoulder is playing. The movie has been on my list of *want to sees* for a long time. Claude Rains performs the part of Satan, who is afraid of heights and who loses in the end. I almost feel sorry for the *poor devil*. The story fills me with hope. The villain turns to good in the end because he's willing to cooperate with God just a little bit. This makes me think of *National Velvet's* wise mother, who says, "What's the use of goodness if there isn't a little bit of bad to overcome?" She has a point. It comforts me to witness someone's resurrection.

March 30, 1947

I say goodbye to Del Rio and Ms. M. I hope to be in the town of Cline by six p.m. About midday, I stand on the shoulder of Highway 90. Chariot's back tire is loose. I'm parked on a lonely, flat stretch of highway, and no one is in sight; just a herd of Mohair goats grazing near the road on the other side of a rundown wood fence.

As I lean over Chariot, I hear the crackling of tires on the gravel shoulder. The sound grows slowly louder. The hair stands up on the back of my neck. I glance up casually to see a flashy yellow convertible coasting to a stop a few feet away. My gut tells me I don't want to talk to the man in the car, not the way I would talk to most people. I straighten up. The man grinds his car to a stop, gets out, and walks toward me. His clothes remind me of how father looked when he went out alone to the movies in downtown San Diego. When the stranger is still a few feet away, I look him straight in the eyes and say, "Isn't it wonderful how, when you're in trouble, God always sends someone to help?"

Immediately, I hand him Chariot's back wheel, giving his hands something constructive to do. Neither of us saying more, he proceeds to replace and tighten the wobbly and worn balloon tire, while I assist demurely. After a short conversation involving the weather, establishing that he's headed to California, he sends me on my way, wishing me *good luck*. Then, winking, he adds,

"You know, you really should be careful of who you talk to, out here alone."

"Thanks, God," I whisper under my breath, while smiling and nodding in agreement with the quickly receding man. The potential for evil causes me to acknowledge God's goodness, which seems to be the most important thing after all. There's hope in this. There is even hope for Father, I think. Shadowy memories flit by of Mother's heavy sigh as our family watches father open the dining room cabinet and take out the bottle of whiskey. Time and again, I hope and pray goodness will overcome Father's need to drink. I want my goodness to help him fight his urge to indulge in a sin. But, he seems to take such pleasure in it, and I'm still not sure what my responsibility is.

Minutes after this meeting, I retire for the night in a goat pasture under the cover of tall, bright-leafed mesquite bushes. At sunset, I stroll barefoot on the green lawn, looking for goats. What is that? A strange-looking creature

roots in the fallen leaves and grass. Should I watch or run? I stay and meet a shy armadillo. He reminds me of a pig with rhinoceros skin as he skitters away, wagging his little pointed tail behind him. We don't have *critters* like this in California!

I lie down for the night. The soft clang of a bell strapped to the neck of the leader of a herd of small white goats comforts my slightly jangled nerves. The mother goat nuzzles me and nibbles my hair to see how I taste. Slowly, I reach out with one hand to touch her full, pink udder, which hangs so low it almost touches the ground. I close my eyes, imagining it is my cat, Sheila, back home, and halfway expect to hear a purr. Sister Juney's first letter to me announced that Sheila had given birth to three kittens, which the family decided to keep! Jealous as I think about my family making decisions without me, words to a silly song pop up in my mind. "How can I miss you if you won't go away?" I miss you, family.

Curious to try warm goat's milk, I move slowly into position, lying under the friendly goat's utter, ready to catch a squirt in my mouth. But before I can yank on her teat, she leaps sideways a few feet as she cocks her head, eyeballing me suspiciously. "Maahhh," she bleats, then tosses her head and trots nonchalantly over to a nearby mesquite bush. Instantly in love with these playful creatures, I promise myself someday to get one, to milk whenever I want.

Before crawling into my sleeping roll for the night, I remember to check for ticks. I gingerly pick off five big ones, severing each head with a quick *crunch* between two fingernails. Then I lie under the tree and eat crackers, cheese, and cold meat, while staring at the myriad of stars that twinkle directly above me. As I stare, a strange thought occurs to me. Do I see stars or are they really holes in the sky that let little bits of heaven shine through? I lay staring and trying to see for sure, tempted to suck my thumb for comfort, since I couldn't pet a goat. Sleep comes quickly to shorten the lonely the night.

Highway 90 flies by. A lithe animal, I eat up the flat miles, passing through small towns, about thirty miles between each one—Uvalde, Knippas, Sabona, D"Anis, Hondo, and on. The vegetation grows more lush and green with each mile I ride east, toward my destination of the big city of San Antonio, where I hope to find work and rest.

Dozens of narrow bridges on Highway 90 ford small creeks, and I laugh at the name of each creek I pass. My favorite is *Woman Hollering Creek*. Of course, I stop and explore the area. Why would a woman be hollering here? I look for clues, but find none. Still curious, I stop to eat dinner at a tiny *shack* of a café a few miles farther down the road.

Ordering a large bowl of chili, I get my first taste of the South, and, I find the *hollering* women. A group of ten college-age Negro women troop in. One by one, they push nickels into the jukebox and begin to dance. They vibrate the joint from its loose shingles to its rotting steps with their *jubilant jitterbugging*. I can't keep my feet still as I watch the floorshow; dark bodies stepping and shaking to rhythmic music, their half-wild shrieks electrifying the atmosphere. I marvel at jangling ankle, wrist, neck, and ear ornaments, and think of Africa. Curious and friendly, a few of the dancing girls eventually tug on my arm to join them. I politely decline, feeling too foolish to try, though I secretly would love to *holler* with them.

Dusk finds me twirling on a merry-go-round in a local park. I don't even care who's watching. I read somewhere in the Bible, that I'm to *put away childish things*, but also to *become as a child* in order to enter *Heaven*. So what should I be, a grownup or a child? God, I don't understand! Suddenly, as I twirl, something breaks loose inside me. *Ping*! Like something stiff with rust, keeping my heart locked up. Is it a shell inside me that has cracked so I can find a pearl? I squirm with discomfort at the thought of changing. Would it hurt to change? What would I become? Questions linger.

As I lay in the center of a field of Texas Blue Bonnets, sweet mockingbird songs lulling me to sleep, I think of the *resurrection fern*. If God nurtures a fern, then He also nurtures me. He finds good even in the bad; I long to have Him find the good in me. Amen.

CHAPTER 10
The Other Side of Texas

April 1, 1947

April Fools day wakes me, dripping in warm, misty rain; Cicadas chirp, "*Shreeeeee. Shreeeeee,*" as if laughing at the joke nature played on me. Another full day of easy pedaling on flat roads, I swish past miles and miles of farmland, then forests.

Sycamores, oaks, pecans, and occasionally a palm or fir. Tall, green, and mighty, they march along the road beside me, saluting with long, leafy arms. Then, as if by magic, San Antonio rises out of nowhere, sprawling as far as my eyes can see. The biggest city I've seen since San Diego, it lay chaotic, random, as if some giant had dumped his building blocks out, and where they fell, there now lay a building.

Following dusty, congested roads toward the towering brick buildings of downtown, I locate the post office, hoping for letters from home.

Lounging in the park next to the Alamo ruins, I read two letters. Neill's neatly written, four-page letter describes, in detail, dating college girls, and finding them quite entertaining. *Heartless brute. Remember the Alamo?* A bold symbol of the Texas heritage of the willingness to die rather than endure oppression. I briefly savor the idea of combat with my coquettish foes.

The other letter is from Mom. Full of trivial things until close to the end; she exhorts me to send something to submit to the *Ocean Beach News*. Apparently, my reading audience is growing, demanding the latest news of my trip. I feel honored and irritated. "Honestly, I didn't know I had a *fan club*. Whose trip is this, anyway?" I grumble.

Feeling the usual shyness, vulnerable now, I reluctantly make a phone call to friends of the Bs, whose number I had kept safely in my little black book. Martha S. answers her phone. "Where have you been? We've been looking for you! Our apartment is at One Twenty Ira Street, and the couch is waiting for you. Stay as long as you want." How did they know about me? Had the Bs told them? I feel faint, overwhelmed by an odd elixir; a concoction of hunger and relief.

I waitress at the Shanghai Café; eighteen dollars per week, plus thirty dollars per week in tips. I've never known a Chinese person before. Sweet and sour, like the food they serve, my fellow workers run short on smiles, but long on kindness. Louie W., the cook who sports a V-shaped mustache in the center of his narrow face, topped by horizontal patches of thinning black hair, introduces me to the pleasure of Shark fin soup. In exchange, I lead bike tours around San Antonio for the Ss and all the restaurant staff.

I find my voice in San Antonio as I encourage others to cycle with me, showing them, by experiencing it, how the bicycle can be our friend. Like a different kind of missionary, I try to put the *romance of the road* under the wheels of my converts. "Whatever you want," I preach, "envision it and the bicycle will help you achieve it. No barriers exist between what we are and what we dream of becoming when we let go of the earth and fly through the universe on our *wheels of salvation*."

The grandeur of Texas heritage flourishes everywhere. Daily, accompanied by my enthusiastic bike buddies, we see it all. Missions, forts, sunken gardens, and the zoo. We even canoe on the San Antonio River and shop for treasures at the Farmer's market. Best of all is the Fiesta. Held once a year, it culminates with the Battle of the Flower Parade, a solemn pilgrimage to the ruins of the Alamo Fort, and coronation of the Fiesta Queen, as grand as if she is the queen of England.

The longer I stay in Texas, the fatter my pocket book grows, and the bigger my visions become. Roots grow quickly when nourished and I'm nourished here. Maybe I'll just stay indefinitely. Passion breeds confidence, they say. As an *athlete extraordinaire*, I feel exempt from society's rules for women. I feel powerful, proud, bigger than life. *Uh oh. Hmmmm ...*

Dash! I wake one morning to a larger than normal dose of shame. Time to call home, now that I can afford to. Time to forgive my mother for nagging.

"Mom, it's me. I'm having a blast in San Antonio."

"Praise God, Norma. We received the candy. Pop likes his cactus. When are you going to write again?" Mom interrogates. She is relentless. I ignore her question.

Then, afraid to ask, but compelled, "How's Buddy?"

"Norma, he's been released from Anthony's. He's trying to turn over a new leaf," Mom answers. I fight back tears as relief and worry choke my throat. He is out, but for how long? What would be different for him?

"Norma, sometimes bad things that happen to us can

be blessings in disguise." Mother is preaching at me again. Mute, I wonder how this applies to Buddy. I know better than to probe deeper, and, many important things left unsaid, we chat about nothings for a few more minutes before I tell her that it's costing me a bundle to call and hang up after saying a polite goodbye.

Why do blessings have to come in a disguise? I grind my teeth in disgust. Blessings should come without mystery or pain, like a *jack-in-the-box*. Turn the handle and eventually a blessing pops up, obvious, staring me right in the face. Is this unrealistic, God? Not that I deserve very many, I confess. God, I promise to be obedient to Mother and write something down for the newspaper soon. Amen.

April 28, 1947

I leave San Antonio ten pounds heavier, a well-rested *lump of lard*, and forty-five dollars richer. Spending another fifty dollars on a new wardrobe at Joshes, San Antonio's largest department store, I mail most of the clothes ahead in a suitcase to Grandmom's house in Baltimore. When I arrive there for Christmas, at least one package will be waiting for me under her tree. They say it's more precious to give than to receive. So I give to myself.

I sleep tonight in a roadside park amid daisies and fireflies. The S. children told me fireflies could light up an entire room with their glow, if caught in a jar. If I break off the tail and put it on my finger, they say it would make a firefly ring. Though tempting, I refrain from testing this hypothesis because it seems unnecessarily cruel. Neither do I pick daisies, knowing they would also quickly die. Better to enjoy beauty as it grows, then leave it for the next person to enjoy. I admire my new maturity. At dusk, I rest, stomach full of fresh goat's milk given to me by a local farmer. Tomorrow, I'll coast into Austin and take the grand capitol of Texas by storm.

Heading northeast on Highway 81, over the graceful city bridge I glide into downtown Austin. The city greets me, a well-groomed brick jungle; Sixth Street booms lively with jazz and booze. I head for broad Congress Street to see the capitol building. Oversized, dazzling in the bright Spring sun, it stands a monument to Texas' wealth, stability, and presumed good taste. I find the YWCA and proudly pay rent for the night, planning to stay only a day before heading to Houston and then Louisiana before the hot weather hits.

Today I pedal the few blocks to Town Lake to swim. Several *anglers* sit half-heartedly swatting mosquitoes and dangling their lines in hopes that a catfish or bass would hook itself. As I search for a spot to wade into the lake, one of them tells me the small, picturesque lake is actually the Colorado River, dammed up before it continues southeast to Houston.

White swans gracefully paddle nearby as I daydream of being Tom Sawyer and Huckleberry Finn rolled into one. Spying an old rowboat, about six feet long, lying capsized in the mud and reeds, my imagination takes wing. I remember vividly from the movie how Tom and Huck create a craft worthy of floating down a river. Why couldn't I do that? I could float to the small town of Bastrop in a day, get back on the road and continue rolling east toward Houston from there!

Pleased with my ingenious plan, I tear the fishermen from their arduous task of lazing around in the cattails. "Can I buy that boat?" They chuckle.

"She's yours if you want her, no charge."

I murmur thanks and speedily take possession of my treasure before anyone has time to change his mind. I wonder why men always refer to boats as *she*. Why are they laughing?

"Everyone is entitled to one glorious piece of folly in their lifetime," said *National Velvet's* very wise mother in one of my favorite movies. This will be *my* bit of folly. Maybe I'll have an adventure worth writing about. Maybe then my mother will say she is proud of me.

Though the shabby skiff's framing seems sound, its bottom planks are shrunken and warped so badly I can put my fingers through the cracks. Making the poor derelict river-worthy again seems hopeless until inspiration pays me a brief visit. I devise a plan to patch the holes. Remembering techniques Pop used when he repaired things in his basement sanctuary, I purchase putty, thumbtacks, and linoleum. The boat is ready by three p.m.!

Pure luxury is mine as I float down the tree-lined Colorado River, Chariot on board. Like on a jungle cruise, I drift lazily using a forked branch as my paddle, waving to people fishing, cattle grazing, turtles splashing into the water from their branch perches. What a life! The moon lights my way until eleven p.m. when, weary but cheerful, I pull up onto a gravel bar to sleep. *Tom and Huck have nothing on me.*

Nine a.m. this morning, I admire my own cleverness as I attempt to create a sail. Just like Tom and Huck, I tie my canvas tarp to a forked branch. Sailing with Neill in the San Diego Harbor had seemed simple. Now, no wind fills my sail as I munch my last banana for breakfast. Not to worry, I'm almost to Bastrop.

By three p.m. still no Bastrop. I round the next bend in the river and the pace of the currents quicken. Too late to change course, I enter rapids and my boat and I begin a terrifying roller-coaster ride on steep, frothy waves. Three big dips turn my craft broadside to the waves, and over she tips, spilling me, Chariot, and all my gear into the angry, racing current. I only hope that no one witnesses how foolish I look splashing and floundering, like a swimmer with amnesia, the lead weight of my waterlogged Pendleton pulling me under. Thanks only to God, it occurs to me to struggle out of my shirt and drag it with me to shore.

Gone are my cooking utensils, flashlight, and all my new clothes. Most desolating; gone is my Chariot. I bravely swim to rescue what I can; my strong arms cutting through the white chops like machetes as I battle a mighty foe. Miraculously, I recover my money, zipped in a clear plastic purse, my sleeping roll, and my Bible.

After spreading my salvage on the grass to dry, I clamber up a tree, which overhangs the spot near where Chariot submerged. I swing from branch to branch like Tarzan, dangling my feet in the brisk current, trying to feel for my drowning friend, wailing, "Bikey, I want my Bikey." Eventually my hands wrench loose and I splash into the river and wash downstream. Stubborn determination overrides clear thinking. I climb out, barefoot on rough rocks, walk back upstream, and repeat this folly twice more.

Hours later, exhausted, I stretch out on my damp sleeping roll, dazed, despondent, and quivering. Two elderly fishermen notice me and saunter over. Shaking, stuttering, I explain my plight, gulping to keep back hysterical sobs. Will they help? I'd die if they laughed!

"There's no way to get your bike out except with hooks, and even then it would be nearly impossible," the tall, thin one comments, stroking his chin.

"Too bad, but it's only seven miles to Bastrop. You'll get there before dark," the short, fat one, says over his shoulder as he hustles toward his car. They speed off together like their tails are on fire, not even offering me a lift.

That did it! I flop back on my bedroll and weep wantonly; my best friend drowned in the rushing rapids. Heartlessly, water rushes over the frame and wheels that had carried me faithfully so far! All the time I'd spent cleaning and repairing, all the money—gone! My *ways and means* sunk in a bottomless hole. Whaaa ... !

"Pride comes before a fall," I hear mother's voice echoing in my head. Mother doesn't believe in praise. She says it discourages us from trying harder. But what is pride? I'm confused. *National Velvet's* mother was proud of her daughter for following her dream. All a child wants is his or her parents' approval, I think. How can that be a sin? I'll have to ask someone soon. Common sense pulls me from my reverie. I wanted adventure, didn't I? Well, I guess I got it! I stop crying. It could have been worse. I should be thanking God for my life; I give myself my own good advice.

Tired, hungry, reflective, I lay down on my sleeping roll

at dusk among a small herd of amazed cows. I sing them a childhood hymn that holds new meaning now. "Ezekiel saw two wheels a-rolling, way in the middle of the air." "Do dead bicycles go to heaven?" The cows do not comment. Is this a blessing in disguise? I doubt it! Finally, I slip into the dreamless sleep of exhaustion.

Bastrop is still seven miles away, so, after shaking the morning dew from my sleeping roll, I stick out my thumb to hitch a ride. Am I invisible? No one even slows down, so I walk. Gravel tears up my bare feet until they look like something that would come out of my mother's hand-powered meat grinder.

On I trudge. Finally, barking dogs announce my arrival as, bone tired, I approach civilization. On the sagging front porch of an unpainted wood shack sits a middle-aged man, sporting bib overalls, rifle in hand. A tiny, wrinkled old woman, wearing her pure white curls like a crown, rocks in her chair beside him, chewing tobacco and spitting into a tin can. She never misses a shot. I hum "Farmer in the Dell" so I can't hear the *ting* of the spittle.

"Come on in," the matriarch invites me with dark-stained lips when I tell them my situation. I look like a *river rat*, my hair hanging in soggy strings, dragging my pitiful belongs behind me. Undaunted, the kind man fixes ham, eggs, and grits while Granny S. fetches me dry clothes. The shapeless housedress she offers hangs like a potato-sack from my shoulders.

"Thanks for the loan," I say. My oversized grin camouflages my annoyance; I look too much like my mother in it.

Staying with the Ss until I find a new bicycle, I share a single cot with two school-age girls. In exchange, I help plow their field and hunt squirrels for dinner. In the evening, the four S. children and I eat berry cake soaked in sour milk and listen to Granny talk of times past. She's full of wisdom. "Don't use the outhouse," she warns. "It's full of spiders. You had best go around the side of the house, like the rest," she advises. Remembering the stories of Brown Recluse, I obey.

The citizens of Bastrop, charmed by my plight, try to outdo one other in generosity. When news of my demise reaches Mr. R., the owner of the grocery store, he instructs me to pick out any pair of shoes I want at the department store; he would foot the bill. I choose a practical pair of black and white saddle shoes and, when I kiss the kind old gentleman on the cheek, he blushes bright red with pride.

"I praise you, God, for your never-ending mercy, even though I don't deserve it," I pray each night.

The Ss find me an almost-new bicycle that I can buy for the bargain price of nineteen dollars. Two weeks after my tragic arrival, my new wheels, Chariot II, and I roll triumphantly toward Houston energized by the thought that I have won the heart of a whole town!

Gosh! The road runs smoother as I travel; my new bicycle cruises faster. The wind at my back for a change, I sail forward. One hundred and thirty-five miles in one afternoon, this is the fastest I've traveled so far. Could the loss of my precious Chariot I be a "blessing in disguise"? Maybe ...

Rain falls gently as I enter the massive city of Houston. Startled Texans stand under awnings and in sheltered doorways watching me ride down Houston streets. But I don't care what they think. I'm Norma Jean Belloff, *Speed-Demon Belloff* they call me back in Ocean Beach. Now, where is that YWCA?

Within minutes, I find the multi-story, red brick building and pay for one night with my river-washed money. Neill on my mind, I hightail it to the main post office, hoping to hear more from him. There is a letter bearing gruesome news. He informs me that he is seriously dating a girl he met at college. He wishes me the same good fortune in the future. Ouch!

Hurt, but not overly surprised, I determine to *take the bull by the horns*. God can talk to me any way He wants. The best bit of blessing, lately, fell out of a Chinese fortune cookie. It read, "Don't pursue happiness—create it!" This is exactly what I intend to do, Texas style. After traversing this state for more than two months, I figure I know how!

I cruise the city streets, absorbing the sights, sounds, and smells. Houston glows with promise for a bright future, like Emerald City, in the land of Oz. Green, the color of money. Cattle and petroleum; it smells like money. Cars honking, sirens screaming, the place teams with rich humanity. Pop would like it here; full of fancy dress and pizzazz. I miss you Pop.

This evening, a gang of girls from the Y invite me to go out on the town. We meander past a myriad of brown, red, and tan brick buildings. Block after block of dance clubs and cafes, music blaring, men staring.

Then, I catch his scent. Some fancy imported men's cologne. Expensive. I turn to look, and there he stands. Tall and dark, he wears an easy smile. Just as any prince should be. We make eye contact. He struts toward me, cowboy hat cocked back, spurs jingling, and introduces himself right there on the sidewalk. His name is Burdett. He mumbles casually, " Your just the prettiest little thing I've seen in all my life." My heart flutters then floats. By the end of the evening, we are an *item*. Was Neill's *Dear John* letter a blessing in disguise? Maybe ...

For the next two days I thrill as Burdett shows me the sights, zipping around on his motorcycle; his life. The port, motorcycle races, museums, and dancing. He's twenty, like me; lonely, like me. We *create happiness* by keeping each other company.

Burdett is a sweet and gentle young *cattleman* with simple desires. On the third day he begs me to stay and marry him. Can people *fall in love* this fast? I feel secure around such an ardent, loyal admirer. He would certainly make a great family man. But, Grandmom expects me in Baltimore for Christmas. Her love pulls me forward, more than Burdett's lavish attention pulls me to stay, so I say goodbye for now.

I promise to write, but try not to encourage him too much, for I now know too well what it feels like to have a heart broken by someone I love. Revenge may be one expression of a woman's grief, but how would hurting Burdett relieve my sorrow about Neill? Deep emotion has no logic in it at all, does it? Yet, perhaps love is more than an emotion. I hope so.

Heading south, I don't want to see the fresh skeleton of Texas City, but the port town is on the fastest route to the Gulf, and I'm desperate for a whiff of the salty sea air. The radios had broadcast the devastating blasts as they happened, twenty-nine days earlier. I had been oblivious; gallivanting around San Antonio with my new friends, and falling in love in Houston, until I saw the newspaper photos. The devastation pictured there was impossible to ignore.

Pedaling quickly through the *remnants* of the town, it lies peaceful now, a memorial to the dead. All color gone. A war zone. The acrid smell of burned life still sifts up from the blackened dirt as I pause briefly to pay my respects. Newspapers reported that five-hundred eighty-one men, women, and children died here, although over sixty bodies remain missing, so badly were they ripped apart. Had I been here a month sooner, I might easily have been one of the curious onlookers who ran to the wharf to watch the colorful chemical-fueled fires. Then I would have been *blown to smithereens* also, when fire ignited ammunition on the ships and in warehouses to create an exploding grave. Is it a blessing in disguise that I tarried in San Antonio and got waylaid in Bastrop? Yes!

Texas City had long been known as a place lonely seamen could go to drink, smoke, and find *love for sale*, but I would never wish this kind of devastation on anyone, no matter how far they had strayed from the narrow path to salvation. Blessings, if any, for the people affected by this disaster, remain hidden under the ashes and deep in grieving hearts. I'm sorry for your loss, Texas City, is all I can think to say.

CHAPTER II
Living and the Dead in Louisiana

May 1947

"Mom, it's me. I finally made it to Louisiana. Although it took me only twenty-two days of travel time to get through Texas, I was actually in that state for seventy days! At times I thought I'd be there forever! Mom," I continue, shouting into the mouthpiece of the old phone at the Acme Café. "All day long I've seen snakes, hundreds of them on the road from Port Arthur. The locals tell me most snakes here are poisonous. Huge cotton mouth, and slim, golden copperhead."

"You probably shouldn't sleep on the ground tonight, Norma. Do you want me to send money ahead to New Orleans for you?" Detecting concern in her voice, shame comes to eat up my glee. I hadn't called home since San Antonio.

"Mom, I told you I'd earn enough money in Texas to keep me going. I really want to try to do this on my own." We both know the truth. I'd accepted help from her and Pop several times already, much to my irritation. Why am I so weak and lazy? God, I know I need help from You.

"How is everyone back home? Pop? Juney? Buddy? Are your headaches better, Mom?" I inquire.

After a long pause on the other end of the line, "Buddy's run off again... . Pray for him, Norma. My headaches still come and go. Everyone else is fine." Mother's voice sounds small and weary. Perhaps it's best not to mention what I'd seen in Texas City. So, we pretend to be okay, exchanging a few more bits of news and then hang up. I feel guilty again, her pain weighs me down like a ball and chain. Am I a headache to my mother?

Chariot and I continue easterly as thick, warm rain pelts my canvas poncho. The mammoth drops make *thuds* on my hood, sounding like my brother Buddy's bee-bee gun pellets as he practiced against the side of our house back home. Buddy, where have you gone this time? When will you be all right?

Winter in Texas had been wet enough. Spring in the South is like swimming in bath water; a real *frog strangler* as the locals call it. When I get thirsty, I just open my mouth and gulp. My saddle shoes and blue jeans are drenched; only my torso feels warm. My calves and ankles ache, chafing against the denim cuffs as I pedal methodically along. I'm determined to reach Lake Charles before nightfall. I've no wish to sleep in the swamp tonight, remembering the writhing mass of snakes along the road.

I arrive in Lake Charles as evening falls. Pedaling through town, I glance longingly into the windows of each home, looking for the right one. Before the rows of houses end, I spot a huge mansion, barely visible from the road. Curiosity and exhaustion overcome me; this might be a good place to look for sympathy.

The massive white pillars gracing the front porch glow under bright lights as I slosh my way up the long driveway. Each inch closer to the house, the stronger a familiar shyness washes over me; the state of wondering, hoping, and worrying all wrapped together into a glob of anxiety. I feel the thrill I always feel when vulnerable and asking for help. Will I find acceptance? Will I win more hearts and gain a new family? Will God be here?

I lean Chariot carefully up against an ancient, moss-covered tree and knock, softly at first then louder, banging the brass, lion-head knocker hard and fast. The door cracks opened after an eternity. Jovial laughter and savory aromas emerge, accompanying the black-haired head of a young woman dressed in a white apron and ruffled cap.

"Hi. I'm Norma Jean Belloff," I say, putting on my most cheerful face. "I'm touring the United States by bicycle and am looking for a place to get out of the rain for the night." This introduction usually does the trick. The greeter, usually a woman, after looking me over, would invite me in with *clucks and tisks* and provide a safe place to eat and sleep for a while. Even though I offer to do work in exchange for room and board, I realize most people consider the recounting of my travel adventures as payment enough. This no longer bothers me. I rationalize that for many, I'm entertainment, like a circus act; something they can tell the neighbors about after I leave.

"I don't know about you, *Missy*. You wait here while I go talk to somebody," she says, then disappears behind the massive white door. There must be a party going on inside, but all I long for is sleep.

The young woman returns with sad news. "I'm sorry, but my boss says we can't have no strangers in our house tonight." With that, the door shut slowly in my face! So much for that famous *southern hospitality*! Too tired to be upset, I return to my rain-drenched bicycle and pedal slowly east on the main road leading out of town.

There are no more lights on the sides of the road as twilight overtakes me, only huge, old moss-draped trees lined up like marchers in some lonely procession that I follow. My eyes can no longer clearly see the sides of the road, when I spot an old wrought-iron gate. Propped half-open, it invites me in. I barely see the letters on the sign above the gate. *Cemetery.*

Neill informed me that a graveyard could be a very safe place to sleep. This makes sense to me. Who else with eyeballs and skin would be *here* at night? There's a first time for everything. So I push Chariot through the gate.

"Anyone home? May I come in?" I ask the graves, the whispering grass, and the silent shadows. Twilight peeks through the fluttering branches of the draping trees. I chuckle nervously and whisper to no one, "I don't believe in ghosts, I don't believe in ghosts," as I tread lightly on the sacred ground. Buddy would love it here! His imagination would run wild, and so would we. We could play hide and seek among the tombs; creeping through the tall grass, screaming like banshees when we find each other.

I trudge down a path between the granite and marble sarcophaguses, standing in stately rows. Flashlight in hand, I inspect the epitaphs, searching for something. All of these dead people have been loved by someone. I look for something more ... I find what I need under the branches of a giant live oak tree. "And when you were dead ... he made you alive together with Him, having *forgiven* us all our transgressions," Colossians 2:13. Forgiveness. That's what I need. I take pleasure in making Mother worry. I deserted Buddy. I can hardly remember what Neill looks like. So many miles away from all of the people I love, I lay my soggy sleeping roll down between two tombs, draping my poncho over them to protect my head from the relentless drops of rain.

Sleep comes quick and merciful. I dream that I sit, warming my toes near the hearth inside the mansion where I'd been turned away. I dream that people dance, merry, twirling all about me laughing and tickling my toes. Later in the night, I wake. Wiggling toes feel colder. Better hold still. The lumpiness of the earth pokes into my back. My nose is cold. The sweet scent of freshly washed air and wet earth fill my nostrils, reminding me of my fern garden back home. I open my eyes. The silhouettes of trees loom blacker than the clear, twinkling night sky.

A dog *ruffs*. A cow *moos*. A single tree frog croaks, "*duuuck, duuuck, duuuck.*" More awake now, I sit up, propping myself on my elbows. Tombs glimmer in the starlight, decaying memorials to ancestors. What bliss there must be in eternal sleep ...

"Aahhhhhh!" I scream, loud enough to wake the dead. Something cold and slick is touching my toes inside my sleeping bag! I scramble out. Nothing comes to mind but snakes, snakes, poisonous snakes! I turn on my trusty flashlight, which hangs on a shoestring around my neck. With one big swoosh I scoop my sleeping roll up side down and shake it hard. What drops to the ground is not a snake, but a huge Louisiana Bull Frog. He squats there, indignant, eyes gleaming in the bright beam of my light. Then he hops away. I laugh so hard that I pee my pants ... just a little. But laughing turns to coughing as I inhale some of the hundreds of early spring mosquitoes swarming around me. Ouch, yuck. I swat and leap back into my bag, hurriedly zipping it closed over my head, only my nose protrudes for air.

I lay waiting for sleep or morning to come. Buddy, are we courageous, insane, or both? Only time will tell. We each run away like the gingerbread man. *Catch us if you can.* Buddy, my heart aches to tell you it will be okay, it's not your fault and all is forgiven. Don't give up, little boy. There's so much more to the world than what you know. God, please show me the way to help him. Amen.

Today, after pedaling forty miles, nothing but soggy bayou on either side of the road, I stop at an elegant plantation located on the outskirts of the small town of Eunice. The friendly family who lives in the mansion, the Ls', welcome me as if I'm royalty. They provide me with a private suite and a personal housemaid. This far exceeds anything I'd imagined. Fantasizing I'm Scarlet O'Hara in *Gone with the Wind*, I waltz from room to room. What glorious satisfaction!

In the morning—bathed, fed, and pampered—I promise to write to them, then continue biking toward New Orleans. What can be done for people who have everything? At noon, I stop to write them a thank you letter, trying to express my appreciation for their generous hospitality. Some believe that spoken or written words are acts. If this is true, I hope my words wrap themselves around the Ls, and hug them tight. God bless them again and again!

CHAPTER 12

Coming Unglued In New Orleans

May 30–June 7, 1947

"A is for Alligator," my nursery primer read. "Want one!" I would tell Mother, poking at the illustration of the *grey-green lizard-looking thing* with my stubby two-year-old finger. As I stare at my first live specimen, sunning all twelve feet of itself on the side of the road, I change my mind. Even though the *gator* wears a permanent crooked smile, like in my picture book, I'd rather see him in a hot soup than in my playpen. I don't even stop to examine the monster closer; I'm told that despite their short legs, they can run at very high speeds. While in New Orleans, I'll shop for a hammock to string between trees when I rest, to keep me out of the toothy alligator's reach.

As I lounge in my bayou boudoir in Houma, Louisiana made private with curtains of weeping willows branches that drape to the ground, I randomly open my slightly moldy Bible and read Deuteronomy 5. The verse describing the sins of the fathers being passed to the children for three or four generations jumps off the page and sticks in my mind like chewing gum on the bottom of my shoe. Sometimes the Bible doesn't comfort me. How does this apply to me?

Visions of death in Texas City still haunt me. I catch myself wondering strange things. Like how long does it hurt when your body is ripped apart by an explosion? At the moment of death, is there time to make one last confession of sins before one's heart stops beating? I need to talk to someone about this, but who can I trust besides God?

What do I expect to find as I ride my Chariot into New Orleans by way of Highway 90? I hope for a reprieve from the heat and humidity. Ha, ha! Way past Mardi Gras it's the beginning of hurricane season. Maybe I'll find John Carroll swaggering there, like I had in Arizona. I wonder if he'd remember me. Probably not.

Thus my brain babbles as I enter New Orleans where the highway becomes South Claiborne Avenue. I screech to a halt at the first sidewalk café in the famous French Quarter and order a giant bowl of shrimp gumbo. Ravenous, I barely chew before gulping it down. Seagulls dive bomb as I eat; they must be starving too. Pigeons bob and coo around my feet where I sit. Peck, peck here, peck, peck there.

A nauseating concoction of smells assaults my nostrils. Salt air, fish, urine, ripe garbage, and diesel fuel from ships docked on the Mississippi River. I almost *lose my lunch.* Queasiness threatens to spoil my day. Like *Humpty Dumpty* who sits on the wall, I think I might fall and break. What is happening to me?

The youthful, caramel-skinned waiter who serves me dinner kindly explains how to find the YWCA. The lilt in his walk titillates me. I'd like to lick him to see how he tastes. "Norma!" I chastise myself. "What's wrong with you?" I ride Chariot straight to the YWCA. The officious young clerk informs me I could stay for four days at seventy-five cents per night, but then would have to give up my room to someone who made reservations prior to my arrival. She offers me a list of rooming houses to investigate. I feel even more unsettled.

Seeking equilibrium, my thoughts focus on money. *Cold cash* comforts me, a tangible form of security. I've got a *nest egg*. Mother would be proud of me. I like the feeling of coins jingling in my purse, and I want more. So, I respond to a newspaper ad for a job at Salazar's Grocery, located at the corner of Royal and Iberville Streets. The ancient two-story buildings all around me in the French Quarter are constructed of brick, plaster, and wood. Painted ice cream colors, each balcony is garnished with railings of licorice-black wrought iron imported from Spain, they tell me.

In the French Quarter, everyone has something to sell. As I peddle bananas and exotic floral bouquets on the sidewalk in front of Salazar's, street vendors serenade me with their crawfish and gumbo jingles. Street urchins, like packs of buzzing flies, plague me to buy their trinkets or to let them shine my travel-weary saddle shoes. One block away, casinos and hot jazz spots are rumored to house illegal gambling, mafia meetings, and prostitution. Even Voodoo religion can be purchased in small shops on almost every block. I don't dare go in one to look around. Locals tell me the queen of voodoo is buried in one of New Orleans' *Cities of the Dead*, which are above-ground cemeteries built to protect the cadavers from floating about during a flood. Am I safe here?

Morning noon and night, crowds of jovial people of all colors flow through New Orleans; on foot, by streetcar, and even horse and buggy. A colorful river of humanity moving along the banks of the mighty Mississippi River. What are they celebrating? Life? New Orleans invites me to be whoever I want to be. Accepting the invite, I try on *new skin* to see how it fits. My second day of work, I wear the *slinky shop girl* skin. Exuding careless sophistication, I stand slouched, with peasant blouse slipping low off one shoulder, eyelids halfway lowered, and lips puckered up like Marilyn Monroe. Although sailors flock to me and buy my flowers and fruit, I feel too small to fill out the skin; it sags in the bosom and behind.

Finally, told to vacate my bed at the YWCA, I find space to room with two other women at a boarding house on Palmyra Street. In the company of my new roommates, I try on the *Budding Artist* skin. W. asks me to sketch her as she stands nude in the doorway of the bathroom after a shower. She is a milky-skinned red head, thirty-three years old, who teaches school in the Miscopy hill country close by. She's in New Orleans for a vacation, she says, but her holiday masks desperation. She fears becoming an *old maid*.

Feigning nonchalance, I sketch her in pencil on a piece of notebook paper. She discretely holds a towel in front of her lower half, but I get the impression from her shy smile that W. enjoys my attention a little too much. I ignore any invitation. This skin fits no better than the last one.

C., my other roommate, appears much older than her twenty-one years. Her heavy makeup, outlandish wardrobe, and *too inviting* smile make people gawk when we stroll the streets. Her thick black hair is over-dressed with *switches*; hairpieces that she yanks out and rudely tosses at W. and me whenever the fancy strikes her. Most shocking is her habit of lying about our tiny apartment completely nude. She explains that her work as an exotic dancer requires her to be immodest. To her benefit, C. has a *keen* mind and cleverly labels us *faith, hope, and charity*. Which one am I?

All three of our aims in life are so different, yet the kindred spirit of adventurous optimism draw us close. Interesting, that when I stay in a place a short while, I quickly become attached to people. We don't waste time with formalities. Perhaps it's easier to be honest when we know we will part ways soon, never to see each other again. Honesty creates trust. Trust creates friendship. Wow! This is important information.

Compelled by curiosity to try on Negro skin, I hop on a streetcar and sit down beside an umber-colored woman near the back of the bus. She smells of rose water, mingled with a scent of baking bread. I couldn't guess her age; the only wrinkles visible are those around her mouth. Those creases had been carved by daily determination to remain undefeated, judging by the way she clenches her large, black handbag. Her shining, jet black hair is smoothed down under a stylish little red hat; a crown of glory. Her presence comforts me, reminding me of my dark-skinned playmates in Hawaii and the friendly Mexicans in San Diego. I long to hug and kiss her and touch her velvet skin.

"How are you, today?" I ask, smiling. To my surprise, she just squirms in her seat a bit, then frowns at me. I look around for the problem. I see a wooden sign hanging from the back of the seat in front of me. In bold letters are painted the words, "For Colored Only." My confused brain struggles to comprehend. What color are they referring to?

Then, I laugh nervously. "Oh, I guess I'm not supposed to sit here."

"No, ma'am!" was her reply. She didn't seem to want me sitting next to her any more than the local white people wanted me to sit there. Disappointed, I move forward in the bus to my *assigned* seating.

Shame washes over me, increasing the rattle I feel inside. How can people live side-by-side and hate each other? Then it hit me. Isn't this the way things are in my own home? There are times when all of us pretend to get along when we really want to kill each other! The blanket of my denial lifts slowly; exposing the naked truth.

Taught all my life to stay away from downtown and sailors, in New Orleans I investigate both. Dave, an apprentice seaman on the British liberty ship, the Maple Bank is stationed in New Orleans for a short while before returning to England. He's my *tour buddy.* Contrary to what my parents fear, Dave remains a total gentleman, not even requesting to hold my hand. We revel in the pleasures of New Orleans together, both strangers in a strange land. He even treats me to a glorious ride on a steam cruiser that provides tours on the Mississippi for less than two dollars per person.

Lake Ponchartrain Amusement Park has just been completed and *Sailor* Dave and I find innocent entertainment there. Complete with roller coaster and swimming area, we *play* all day. The Wonder Club sits at the foot of West End, and hangs over the edge of the expansive lake. Thinking it another childish amusement, I want to see it. None of my newfound friends object or tell me more about it, so we all go.

All evening we sip drinks and view shows performed by

female impersonators. How could men look so beautiful and act so feminine? The shows, full of suggestive dancing and bawdy jokes, are aimed at their main clientele; other men! Although the impersonators' behaviors seem bizarre to me, they are also disturbingly familiar. Where had I seen this before? Like a tiny worm wiggling up from underground, the disturbing answer comes to my consciousness. The male performers remind me of my Father when he is drunk!

I've come unglued! My mind swirls in a vat of moral confusion. I find myself questioning everything I've been taught about right and wrong! Wandering alone around town, I search for something to remind me of what I believe in; to remind me of God. I pass by the Saint Louis Cathedral every day on my way home from work. The towers of the church, like a fairy castle, cast pointed shadows on the Jackson Town Square each evening. Today I need church, so I go inside.

Sweet choir singing greets my sorry ears; soft light illuminates the massive room. The vaulted ceiling extends all the way to Heaven. Everything here smells of exotic incense and spiritual antiquity. People sit or kneel in the long wooden pews, facing the elaborate shrine at the end of the long aisle. There are no *segregation* signs, so I settle in the back pew where Negroes sit. No one of any color expresses objection.

As I lower myself onto the little *knee bench,* I realize I know nothing about the Catholic Church. Do we worship the same God? Glancing about at the many statues and paintings of saints and angels, I don't see Jesus anywhere! Disappointed, I quietly rise and slip into a side hall then out the back entrance.

There, in the warm, soft glow of evening light, I find *Him*. A statue of Jesus, carved in white marble, faces away from the church and towers above me, arms outstretched. His palms turned toward heaven, He blesses the garden paths and boxwood hedges around Him, beckoning to all to turn their hearts to Heaven for comfort. Under the statue is engraved *The Sacred Heart of Jesus*. Peace comes to me here. God, I know you will not let me fall ... Amen.

I can't believe Burdett is here in New Orleans! He insists I spend time with him so I alter my plans and stay an extra day. Pledging his heart to me again, he promises that when I return to San Diego he will move there to work, *woo* me, and marry me. I must admit, I enjoy the flattery and his devotion is heartfelt. Deep down, though, I don't think he would be able to offer me enough to make me happy. Happily ever after, like in the fairytales of my childhood. Is this too much to ask for, God?

We part again with promises to write, but nothing more. I'm sure he imagines he will marry me, so enamored is he. But, it's not my fault, is it? Whose happiness am I responsible for, anyway? I pray I haven't given him false hope so that his heart will break. God help me. I have wicked thoughts and desires. Save me from myself. Amen.

Chariot and I finally take to the road again, but I'll never forget New Orleans. The truth revealed to me there cut like a hot knife, melting seams carefully fused together by myself and my family when I was very young. Partially removed are many of my childish fantasies, which I no longer need. Fantasies—my family is perfect; if I'm good, then only good things will happen to me. I found life in New Orleans to be complicated, not black and white, and this reality pushes me closer to God, whom I cling to with all my might. But, if it is true as it says in Deuteronomy, that the father's sins are passed down three or four generations, what hope do I have for redemption? Jesus, only You are my rock that cannot be moved. Amen.

CHAPTER 13
Perspective in Mississippi and Alabama

June 1947

"Windy again," I whine to Chariot's deaf ears. Traveling Highway 90 across the divide between Lake Ponchartrain and Lake Borgne, the sea breeze beats against me like Mother's broom against her braided rag rugs when she hangs them on the clothesline. *Whap! Whap!* Pedaling harder and gaining less ground, the resistance to my effort is like a giant hand pushing against the front of my bike. Like trying to swim through a river of mud, the pedals move around, my muscles sting with the effort, but I stay in one place.

The wind here is different from the desert. Constant, relentless, it smells of salt and fish. I stop every few hundred yards to catch my breath. Phooey, *ppphhpt*! I inhale a bug. It flutters, I fear forever stuck in my throat. Trying unsuccessfully to cough it up, I bravely swallow. Pop would say the bug is a little extra protein for my diet, but I worry that it might be poisonous. Too late now!

Bridges on this Gulf Coast terrify me. In the desert, they offer shelter from the sun and rain; a place to sleep hidden from other travelers. Now on this narrow ribbon, there are large bodies of water on either side. I share the bridge with mechanical beasts that roar past, sometimes inches from my shoulder ... and I have no place to go!

There's a song for every occasion in life. I need to sing now, so I hum with my lips sealed tight, saying the words in my head.

> *Got any rivers you think are un-crossable?*
> *Got any mountains you can't tunnel through?*
> *God specializes in things thought impossible—*
> *He does the things others cannot do.*

Thank you, God. Amen. I relax. Dusk descends and I stop to rest in Fort Pike State Park near the Pearl River in Mississippi. How is it possible to travel only seventeen miles in two days?

New Orleans, with its charm and intrigue, held me captive for seven days. Back on the road, I'm still broke; most of my hard-earned cash gobbled up by a new bundle of clothes! So much for traveling light! In fact, I accumulated so many garments that I purchased a suitcase, filled it until near explosion, and mailed it to Jacksonville, Florida, care of general delivery. I hope it will be there when I arrive.

Mom, I may never catch on to how to build a nest egg. I may just remain an egghead instead.

Wahla's Service Station owner takes pity on me when I arrive both wind-tattered and starving. He says I can work for him eight days' pumping gas, while his regular worker is on vacation. Sleeping for free in the back room of his shop, within a few days, I look and smell like a *grease monkey*.

Mr. W. trusts me enough to drive his car to the town of Slidell, eight miles away, to buy groceries. This is the first time I drive a car since San Diego and the voluminous black Buick seems like a gargantuan boat, floating smoothly down the asphalt stream. I strangle the giant steering wheel—peering over the top and through the narrow windshield, the winding road barely visible—and flinch every few seconds, fearing we will collide with the bushes on either side. I much prefer the view from the seat of my bike where I can actually see tires touch the road! Oh, well.

June 22, 1947

I set out again with a week's wages and a few cans of food; rain variable, temperature sweltering, and humidity drenching! As usual, I just follow my nose to see what will happen. Although I eventually plan to cycle to Baltimore before I head home again, this time my nose leads me to a Gulf Seawall, east of the Bay of Saint Louis; Pass Christian, Mississippi. This will be my private, outdoor bedroom. Spreading my woolen blanket out on the second-to-the-bottom stair of the eight-stepped cement dyke, I prepare to sleep on the edge of a continent!

Wow! What a different perspective I have, lying on the shelf and peering about. In New Orleans, the seagoing ships, docked inland on the Mississippi River, tower above the houses and trees, looming huge, like some oddly shaped skyscrapers. Now, ships appear dwarfed; far out to sea, they're but shapeless dots on the horizon, like tiny tufts protruding from the folds of a deep blue quilt. God, I want to live my life like this ocean. Infinite with possibility ...

Night falls. No humanity in sight, I lay on my side and gaze out to the horizon where the heavens and sea merge.

Above me hangs a shifting panorama of stars, clouds, and moon. Occasionally, the lights from heaven are caught by the dancing sea, trapped for a moment before escaping. A lighthouse beacon, far away and almost over the horizon, flickers like a firefly. The lapping wavelets caress my mind, Hush, hush hush. My eyelids droop. The sea air sooths my nostrils and the constant breeze protects me from eager mosquito hordes. From inland wafts the sweet fragrances of warm, wet earth and spring foliage, complimenting the stanza of nature's lullaby that folds gentle arms around me, leading me to tranquil sleep. *Rock ... rock ... rock.*

I wake about one a.m. (according to my waterproof watch) to find a storm brewing. Torrents drop as I run to seek cover in a wall-less beach hut a few hundred yards away, dragging my bike and bedding with me. The wet wind blows through the hut and soaks my blanket, so I drowsily work my wet body down into my waterproof sleeping roll. Disregarding the pounding drops and thrashing storm around me, I pursue slumber again, only to dream that I'm sitting in our claw-foot bathtub back home, floating Buddy's toy boat.

A fresh, calm dawn wakes me, and I continue my gypsy journey. I wonder if I'll ever be dry again! My hair and belongings sag, stained dark green with mildew, as they were before New Orleans. I feel like a bedraggled mermaid, or worse, something slimy, dredged from the bottom of a swamp.

June 23, 1947

I reach Mobile, Alabama, by dusk. Because the sky hangs

thick with rain clouds and hungry mosquitoes, I ride slowly, looking for a house with a screened-in porch. The first door I knock on is opened by a little, white-haired woman who politely waits until I finish my first sentence. "No!" she says, emphatically. I wonder what I look like from her perspective.

Undeterred, I try the next house. "May I sleep in my roll on your porch?" I ask, then quickly add, "You see, I usually sleep outside, but it looks like rain and there are so many mosquitoes here." The plain but attractive young woman stands like a statue, staring at me for many seconds before she noisily sucks in air.

"What did you say?" she asks, re-buttoning her cotton shirtdress, smoothing the rumples in her threadbare skirt. I explain again. "Well, that's an unusual request!" Glancing around, she continues. "The porch wouldn't be much protection from mosquitoes. The children have the screens poked full of holes." I talk quickly, working hard to make charm ooze from my sweaty pores so that she will say *yes*. The porch looks perfect to me, saggy boards and all. Then, she laughs. "My, we've never had such a strange request! You took my breath away at first. I'll go ask my husband."

I won her over! But did she guess that I want more than protection from the elements? Like Goldie Locks, I want to try out all the chairs in their house—the papa, mamma, and baby chairs, to see how each one feels. Besides having a safe place to sleep, I hope to get know another nice family. We will *walk a mile in each other's moccasins* and gain new perspectives from each other, as has happened many times already on my trip. As a result, perhaps, I'll miss my family a little less and be able to love them a little more when I return. This is my dream.

After three days with this young family, I leave. The mother begs me to write and let her know how I am. I smile, wave, and pedal away, mentally adding them to my growing list of families who love me.

As I ride, mile after lazy mile, I daydream, remembering what Mother often said. "We make time for what is important to us." She usually reminded me of this when I neglected to do a chore.

"I have too much to do," I would whine in reply. *Daydreaming*, however, had been my best subject in school. I always seemed to have time for that. While I like to think, I really don't like to write, and haven't written Mom and Pop since Louisiana. I wonder if they feel neglected and unimportant. I'll write, rather than call; phone calls are so expensive.

July 3, 1947

Dear Mom,

How tall does our corn grow in San Diego? Seems like I remember it being five feet tall. I'm standing now in an Alabama field of corn, and it reaches a good three feet above my head. The air is still, and I listen in the silent rows for sounds. At first I can't hear a thing; then, one by one as I listen harder, sounds come; a whippoorwill's clear call from the white-patched blue sky; a clacking cricket conversation from knee-deep patches of grass; a fly's steady drone as he circles about me, looking for a vulnerable spot; human voices, unfamiliar, bohemian, from the nearby farm; the faint, low hum of the tractor loosening earth in the next field for sweet potato planting.

Suddenly, the spell broken, noisy turbulence surrounds me. A gust of wind whips the field into motion. Like a giant horde, the rows of cornstalks bobble, their many arm-like leaves wavering in a grotesque oriental dance. Straw-colored tassels shake like frowzy-haired heads. Sharply, I remember a naked savage mob I saw in a newsreel once, dancing for the royalty of England on their African visit. Then the racket of the thrashing leaves subsides with the wind, and so do the cornstalk personalities. Now I'm among a whispering crowd. Thick stems, like green-haired arms rise from the soil. Tassels, like open hands, plead heavenwards for life from the sun and rain. From a rustling, dark green gown, I pluck a sheathed cob of opulent grains. Their milky sweetness crunches in my mouth. Ummmm!

I feel diminutive in these long, emerald halls. Life's possibilities seem endless. I let my mind wander to imagine what I might do and become. It is delightful, like my childhood game of drawing an outline in the sky with my finger and then watching to see what clouds come to fill it. God, it is good to be alive. It is a relief to feel like a tiny pebble in your giant world, because all my problems and mistakes don't seem quite so big either. I like God's perspective best ...

Love, your neglectful daughter,
Norma

If written words are acts, I know these words will help. I mail the letter, after licking the edge and sealing it with a kiss.

Lounging on a park bench, barefoot, in my shorts and halter, I re-read my letter from Mom when an ominous red station wagon, *POLICE* boldly printed on the sides, pulls up beside me.

"Young lady, you'll have to come with me right now," the stern-looking police officer informs me. Not comprehending, I stare blankly, blinking to see if he is real. After a few seconds, he moves steadily toward Chariot, lifts him up with a powerful swoop, and places him *not so gently* in the back of his vehicle. Next he approaches me just as swiftly, grabs me by my arm, and escorts me to the back seat of the *paddy wagon*, separated from the front seat by wire mesh. Still not comprehending, I stare out the window of my unwanted cab. What can one say in a situation like this? I pray silently, hands tightly clasped and head bowed. God, what have I done? Please protect me.

Downtown Pensacola, I'm deposited like *flotsam* in a sweltering jail cell the size of our bathroom back home. Two bare cots and a seat-less toilet crowd me. The nauseating smells of urine and dirty socks make me gag. Thoughts of rats and cockroaches crawl around my mind; there's not enough light to see what inhabits the cement floor.

"I'm Norma Jean Belloff. Please look at this," I say, standing, stuttering and trying to hand the hard-nosed jailer the newspaper article I'd received from my mother this morning. The article from the paper back home describes who I am and what I 'm doing. Proof that I'm legitimate. Mom, how had you known I would need it?

"Do you know anyone here in Pensacola?" the jailer asks, ignoring the paper.

"I can't say that I do, sir," I reply, numb. Why did he dump me in a filthy jail cell with a *real convict*? I cautiously glance sideways to see a middle-aged woman squatting in a dark corner, scratching her legs, monkey-style. She rocks back and forth from toe to heel, moaning softly. Clothed in a dirty sackcloth dress, she stinks like father did after *falling off the water wagon*, as Mom tactfully said; when he went on *a drunk*.

What has she done, murdered someone? Warned all my life to stay away from *crack-brained idiots* like her, there's no way I can stay here. I'm not that bad! As I sit down gingerly on the cot furthest from my cellmate, a small knot develops in the pit of my stomach; shame travels, like an ice cube, up my spine, and a hollow feeling swallows me.

"Bad girls must be punished!" A stern and critical voice echoes inside my head. Uninvited, a list of *unforgiven* sins from all twenty years of my existence scrolls down the back of my eyelids. With a lead heart, no place to run, I read the list as it plays like the acknowledgements at the end of a tragic movie. Selfish, rude, dishonest, lazy, and disobedient. I'm guilty on all counts. My family can attest to this.

My worst sins are sins of *omission*. *Not* doing something is an action too, isn't it? Like not watching Buddy when we played outdoors. "Don't let him go in your father's shop," mother warned. I was fourteen; Buddy, ten. Mother worried too much. What could happen to him? Pop was in there working, after all.

Eventually, even darker things flutter to the edge of my consciousness, like flies buzzing around something dead. Other things about Buddy; why did he run away from home? Things about my father, ancestral sins, passed down for generations. Things I don't want to understand.

Fear and hopelessness pull me down deeper than the bottom of the Carlsbad Caverns. Intolerable, I try a trick I learned long ago to pull me out of the pit. Squeezing my eyelids together tightly, I fantasize I'm Shirley Temple, my hero; *little miss perfect*. "On the good ship, lollipop, it's a sweet trip into bed I hop ..." jingles in my brain. I envision her brunette curls bobbing as she dances to the melody. Her dimples deepen as she shows her perfect, pearly teeth. Her eyes squint in innocent delight at the thought of a "happy landing on a chocolate bar." For a moment, my trick works; fear slinks back to its corner for a rest before the next round.

In a gentler tone the arresting officer asks again. "Do you know anyone here in Pensacola? I slowly shake my head, no. "It's not right for young ladies to be traveling alone," he says. Pulled from my trance, I glance up to see rings of perspiration staining his uniform under his arms as he lifts his hat and wipes his brow with the back of his arm. The muscles around his eyes and mouth twitch as he returns to his cluttered desk to stare at his papers. Does he regret arresting me?

"He doesn't care," I say under my breath. "I could die in here and no one would know." My well of grief threatens to overflow. Any second I may join the drunken woman next to me in her endless lamentation. I clamp my teeth tight together to control the impending emotional storm, clenching my fists so tight my fingernails nearly perforate my sweaty palms. I hang my head in shame.

"What are you in here for, honey?" my cellmate spits her words, filling my nostrils with her fermented breath as she leans close to me. I wince against the pressure of her dirt-caked hand as it touches my shoulder. I glance up to see her face and stare, riveted by her pathetic grimace. Deep in her weary brown eyes. Is that compassion? She grabs me tighter, awaiting my answer. As she holds, she strokes, and a sooth-ing tingle enters my shoulder and shimmies its way across my chest, bathing me in an unnatural calm. At this moment, all fear vanishes!

"Be still and know that I am God," the calm says. Psalm 46:10. Gradually, freedom envelopes me. Unfettered, I imagine I float right out the window and walk on top of the billowy clouds. When your heart is free, your mind can fol-low! Suddenly, I have an overwhelming urge to bounce up and down on my dingy cot, the way Juney and I used to do when we were small. I want to giggle, a smile as big as the Texas sun stuck to my face, Wow! Who would have thought I could feel free? In a jail, no less!

Still relaxing in her touch, I close my eyes. Is she a *sin eater*? I had read a Scottish tale long ago by Fiona MacLeod, part of Mom's rummage sale collection of obscure literature. The author describes people who took the sins of others upon themselves to relieve both the living and the dead of their pain. Perhaps this notion is *far fetched*, but I wish I could give this feeling of peace and freedom to my family and the world, as my jail mate apparently did for me. Can I do that, God?

As quickly as she had grabbed me, the woman darts back to her corner to continue her moaning and wailing ritual. Did this really happen? Hope and strength from God stays with me.

The jail glows brighter now, seen through the eyes of hope. I find my voice. "Excuse me, why am I here?" I ask the jailer. He sits, back turned to me, in his swivel chair, feet propped on his desk, face close to a small fan spinning at its highest speed.

"Indecent exposure and vagrancy," the jailor says matter-of-factly without turning around. His voice echoes eerily in the vibrating fan. I don't know exactly what he means. "Don't you know anybody in our city?" he repeats, as he slowly stands then strolls closer to my cell. I glance to where my lonely Chariot leans against the wall of the jail, just out of reach. All my possessions are there, forgotten until now.

"Angel, I know of an Angel!" I say, rising and beginning to hop from one foot to the other, doing a Scottish jig. "Please look in my backpack. There's a diary in the front pocket."

"An angel, that's a good one!" He chuckles as he hands me the tattered black diary through the bars. Opening my precious little address book, the note falls out. The handsome young motorcycle rider I met in New Mexico, who had given me his tire pump and encouragement, also gave me his sister's phone number. Her name is Angel. How had he known I would need it?

While I dial her number, the jailor watches, skeptical. Angel flies into action, no questions asked. Although living on a tight budget working at the same motorcycle shop as her brother, within a few hours she manages to scrape together enough nickels and dimes to pay my fifty-dollar bail. Hurray! I don't have to spend the night in jail!

When the *drunk* woman is released, where will she go? A different kind of angel, she had nourished my spirit. I want to say goodbye before I leave the jail, but she finally sleeps peacefully, so I blow her a kiss instead.

I follow Angel home, me on Chariot, she on her motorcycle. When we arrive, I find her apartment so spotlessly clean, I think I'm in heaven. Like sisters, we talk into the night, exchanging secret dreams while braiding each other's hair. She nurtures the same joy of living that her brother does, and I feel blessed to know them both.

The next day, nine a.m. sharp, I stand in court wearing the offending white sun suit; the one I bought in New Orleans. What will my fate be? The stout grey-haired judge proceeds.

"Concerning indecent exposure," he looks me over. "In my opinion, you are covered no less than most Pensacola youth. Not Guilty." "Concerning vagrancy, what are your plans for work here?" He leans closer to me. Perhaps he is hard of hearing.

"Well, sir, I intend to leave Pensacola immediately and secure a job as soon as I get to Jacksonville." I hope this is the right answer.

"All charges dismissed," he pounds the gavel with finality.

I'm free again! "Thank you for everything, Angel. I'll pay you back as soon as I can," I say as we leave the courthouse.

"I really had no choice, Norma. You see, God put you in my way." She grins the same secret grin her brother did, and I accept her explanation with only foggy understanding. Goodbye *my* Angel.

As I set off for Tallahassee, I remember my pastor's voice clearly, "Living in hope is like a prayer to God." Now I begin to understand what he meant. Perhaps I can live more hopefully, knowing God has forgiven me. "Go and sin no more," Jesus says to the woman in John 8:11. Perhaps I should forgive myself. But I'm not sure how.

Chapter 15
Discovered in Jacksonville

July 31, 1947—a date to remember

I'm so near the end of my journey eastward! Energy renewed, I whiz by mile after mile. Strange names pop up on signs as I speed ahead. Apalachicola, Sopchoppy, before the Ochlachome River. I have no way of knowing what awaits me in Jacksonville, Florida. I'm hoping that there will be a letter and money from Mom, so I can buy a mosquito-proof hammock, but that's all I expect, besides getting my first peek at the Atlantic Ocean.

6:30 p.m.

I'm finally here, *smack-dab* in the middle of Jacksonville, a city that appears to be floating on the water that surrounds it. This certainly rates a long distance phone call home, so I start toward a phone booth. But, as I do, I notice a group of people running towards me. After months of travel, publicity increasing as I cross each state, I can identify newspaper reporters from a half mile away. Someone had tipped them off about when I might arrive. Was it Mom?

"Welcome to Jacksonville, Norma. How about letting us get a picture?" says a young woman, camera posed in hand.

"I'd like to make a long distance phone call to my mom, first. I'll just be a few minutes," I say.

"Leave the door open, kid, so we can hear you."

"Are you going on from here, Norma?"

"Operator, I want to call Ocean Beach, California, Bayview four, four—" I shout above the growing din.

"Get a picture of her right now, Charley."

"Let the poor kid get her phone call through," the woman reporter yells.

"That's right. Yes. Yes, collect." I'm panicking now.

"By the way, how much did the trip cost you, Norma?"

"Move back so I can get a picture of her bike!"

"Hello? Mom ... Hi, Mom. Well, I made it. That's right. Here I am in *little old* Jacksonville. Mom, I think there are half a dozen other people in this phone booth with me, so don't mind me if I sound confused. I just got here, and some reporters seem to want to hear every word we say, so I'll just let them hear me say that I think you're the *swellest* Mom in the world for letting me make this trip, and now that I'm really at the goal I set for myself, I appreciate you so much more ..." I want to ask if Buddy has come home yet, but it's too personal for reporters' ears to hear.

Crushed in on all sides by fans, I've no choice but to answer questions, pose for photos, and sign autographs. This continues for an hour and then quiets down a bit. I ask where the YWCA is and hop on Chariot to get there in time to secure a room and a shower for the night. As I bicycle down the street, the crowds follow me on foot, by car, and by bike. Smiling shouting and waving, I'm caught up in the excitement of my success. People had been waiting in the streets for the last few days, hoping to see me as I rode in. I guess I'm famous now, at least around here, and it feels odd in a scary, strange, and even nice way—all at once. Is this how movie stars feel?

The next morning, early, I make a beeline for the mailbox. There are letters from Mom, Jean, Burdett, and Neill; Neill's engaged! There also waits my overflowing suitcase of clothes I'd mailed from New Orleans. Now what will I do with them? Store them, I guess.

Offers of places to stay come pouring in, now that I'm famous. My next destination is Miami, Florida, where I hope to find work for a month. South of Jacksonville I accept an invitation to stay at a great plantation house with a lawyer and his wife. He's the classic southern gentleman; sociable, easy-going, and aristocratic. His wife is what I would call *an oddity*. This sweet and hospitable woman is a *dipsomaniac*; the polite term for one who has the uncontrollable craving for alcoholic liquors. She sleeps until late morning and goes to bed early, sipping away at her *remedy* in between.

The lawyer wants to discuss a paper he's writing on race relations. People think I look sixteen years old but talk with me as if I'm middle-aged. Why?

"The people up north think we mistreat the Negroes; we don't," he says as we sit in the swinging sofa on his front porch. "My workmen are happy," he informs me, as if he's arguing a case. I'm not convinced.

I argue back. "Negroes are individuals with the right to develop as such. Why shouldn't they own some of the orchards and farms?" He doesn't have a rebuttal to my query. Instead, speaking almost to himself,

"A white man doesn't know what he's missed, if he hasn't had a colored man's Saturday night." His eyes glaze over and his lips puff out creating an imbecilic smile, drool dripping from the corner of his mouth, as he stares at nothing in particular. Hearing more than I want to about his personal habits, I quickly change the subject and decide to *head on down the road* in the morning.

As I leave, heading south on Chariot the next day, both he and his wife warn me to *be careful* of Negroes. I don't bother telling them how many times I'd already trusted Negroes during my life. I doubt they would believe me. Instead, I smile and wave, thanking them for their many kindnesses to me. To God I express gratitude that I'd been raised to judge people by their actions and not by their color. Amen.

As I head for Miami, my next destination, I realize that, in spite of my newfound fame, I haven't changed much. My feet still feel the pulse of the things they touch. My toe tips still tingle from what they learn; my hair still finds pleasure, riding on the wind. My blood still loves to *brag* of its color in my cheeks. My body, as always, responds a hundred fold to stimuli around it, making me just *want to jump over the moon* from the thrill of it all. This, after all, is why I ride a bicycle!

The Atlantic air invigorates me, filling my lungs with salt and confidence, and as I move forward, all things seem possible. "I'd give my eye teeth for a place in the pre-Olympic competitions that are happening next spring," I say. The seagulls over my head scream *chree, chree* in reply. Then, they join the pelicans and Blue Heron cranes wading in the estuaries on either side of me as I ride south east on Highway 90.

Mother's response to my *Olympic* idea would be, "What will be, will be." Brother Don would apply his new philosophy and say, "All things are interrelated and preordained."

Although I'm tempted to be fatalistic myself, my prayer is, "May I do your will, God, and if I can affect my fate, Heavenly Father, please show me how." Amen.

Chapter 16
Florida Hurricanes of the Curious Kind

August-October 1947

Oy vay! (Oh my). I should have left Miami and headed north to Maryland sooner, but curiosity holds me captive. I'm curious about *God's Chosen People* and I want a firsthand experience with the mysterious Jewish race. I answer an ad in the paper for a companion-nurse to an eighty-five-year-old Jewish matriarch. I fear my big bones, blonde hair, and blue eyes will betray my German ancestry and I won't be hired. I wonder if I'll be forgiven for the sins of my ancestors across the sea. Belloff could be a Russian name, I reason to ease my nerves. As it happens, Mrs. S. loves everything Russian and she hires me. In the end, I let her come to her own conclusions about my heritage.

Mrs. S.' daughter, B., and son-in-law live in the apartment with us, but they leave the daily personal care of Mrs. S. entirely to me. Unfortunately, Mrs. S. and I butt heads immediately; she's pampered like a queen by her relatives, I'm equally self-absorbed, full of Shirley Temple fairy tales and bigheaded from my recent claim to fame. How silly we must look, two prima donnas vying for first prize; there can only be one winner, and we both know we're right.

I despise having to wake with her at seven a.m. to prepare her morning tea. If I'm not chipper and smiling, she scolds me for being lazy and ungrateful. She glares at me through her thick, wire-rimmed glasses, her tiny four foot-seven-inch tall frame shuddering and her head full of bushy, white hair tilting back as she chides me with her high-pitched cackle. Like the witch in *Hansel and Gretel*, she whines her disapproval of my uncooperative attitude and improper procedures for serving her.

Evenings are the worst. "How many times must I tell you, Norma, the water must be warmed up after you take it out of the ice box ... room temperature, otherwise my heart medicine will not absorb correctly." She barks so that I want to take her by her sagging white throat and strangle her.

"Yes, *Mother S*," I acquiesce, biting my tongue in an attempt to keep from snapping.

"First, off with my jewelry, then my dress, otherwise my jewels will snag the silk." "Waste not, want not," she tells me for the umpteenth time. After carefully removing watch, rings, bracelet, necklace, bosom pin, and earrings, on goes the cold cream; I smear it generously over her wrinkled face, wanting to glue her mouth shut with it so she can't scold me again.

"Norma, shoes on the shoe tree. I will wear my pink brocade slippers tonight. Yes, yes those are the ones. Hurry, my feet are cold. Put the potty closer to the bed, Norma. Put a glass of water on the table next to my cute little puppy dog night lamp. Don't forget to set my alarm. Spray both pillows and the sheets with insect repellent. Norma, massage my scalp tonight after you take down and plait my hair, I have a terrible headache. Don't forget to place the Kleenex under the left corner of the right pillow. Remember to wash out my stockings after you bring me my milk ... not too hot this time, Norma. When will you ever learn?"

Then, after taking a deep breath, Mrs. S. transforms into a silver-haloed angel and coos, "Norma, tell me *sweet dreams*. You know my daughter always used to do that when she would help me. Will you be going to bed now or later?"

My bed is on the couch a few feet away from her, but I often stay up to write after tucking her in. Locking myself in the tiny bathroom, toilet for a seat, I write to myself, to God, and to Mom. My own hand washed slips and towels hang to dry on the Venetian blind cords, because Mrs. S. uses the shower rod as an extra clothes rack; the spacious closet in her bedroom can't possibly hold all her matronly dresses, which reek of mothballs and stale perfume.

Sundays are my day of respite. After helping Mrs. S. with her morning routine, I *fly away* on Chariot, usually to explore the beach. The weather is mild both day and night, and a tropical paradise waits in a grove of palms along the sea wall that separates sand from grass. On the tan shoreline, edged with hotels and castles for the rich, you can see anything and everything in the way of the human form; all shades of brown, red, and white, in all possible poses, dotting the shore. I doddle until dark, picking and eating coconuts and snorkeling many yards from shore, hoping to get a glimpse of bottom-feeding sharks.

After two weeks of self-restraint, I snap. "You don't pay me enough for all I do for you, you nagging old biddy," I blurt. We fight every minute today until she fires me out of frustration. I'm in shock. No one else on the whole trip has turned me out of a home once I'd been accepted in. However, I beg to stay, unwilling to admit defeat due to my own selfishness, and she generously gives me a second chance. In the process, I realize something very important; decision-making without calm is wrong and usually leads to confusion. I tuck this hard- earned knowledge away in my memory for future reference.

I realize that my best remedy against irritation with Mrs. S. is to quickly bring to mind that this might easily be my mother forty years from now. This line of reasoning works like a charm, allowing me to cool down and become loving again.

Just as I've thrilled at conquering a mountain range or a desert on my bike, I find it thrilling to defeat a mental obstacle. Using self-discipline in social interactions brings balance to my life. "Lord, save the pieces," I beseech daily. Perhaps there's hope for me yet!

The other reason I linger longer in Florida is to witness a hurricane. In selfish ignorance, I pray a hurricane will land right in Miami.

Thursday, September 11, 1947

My prayers are partly answered. A double-eyed terror is discovered in the Atlantic.

Tuesday, September 16

Officials announce the hurricane will strike farther north. I think of jumping on Chariot and tearing north to catch it. However, in *bondage* to Mrs. S., I can't leave Miami.

Wednesday, September 17

Suspense draws tight as a glove over everything as the S. household and Miami prepares for a predicted direct hit. Anticipation permeates the atmosphere; some residents fearful, some skeptical, some naively curious like me. In careful preparation, the S. family, our neighbors, and I close shutters, roll up awnings, bolt on metal sections of window-pane protectors, stock cupboards with food, fill bathtubs with drinking water, and clear yards of everything move-able. Volunteers move whole families out of flimsy homes and into fortified public buildings.

Only the mystical *Mezuzahs* remain, hanging outside the front doors of all the Jewish homes. These intricately carved, five-inch metal cylinders, clanging in the wind, contain the symbols of the Jewish faith. I committed to memory the words written on them in Hebrew.

> *Hear, O Israel The Lord is our God one Lord:*
> *And thou shalt love the Lord thy God with all*
> *thine heart, and with all thy soul, and with all thy*
> *might.*
>
> *Deuteronomy 6:4–5*

Also dangling from chains around the neck of each Jew, the *mezuzahs* are a public testimony of their faith. Only two years since the end of World War II. Would I be as brave and open if my race had been attacked by a vengeful regime? I don't know.

Now we're preparing for a different kind of battle. I thrill to be a part of it. Although feverish with activity, compassion flows among the people, a kind of tender forbearance as exits in some families where each member is dearly loved, regardless of character.

A tingle rollicks in the pit of my stomach. Each little gust of wind outside our locked windows flutters stronger than the last. There is no sudden wall of wind as I thought there might be ... only gusty drafts, gradually increasing in strength. My curiosity will soon be satisfied

Thursday, September 18

My chance comes. B. asks me to buy more butter, bread, and medicine for Mrs. S. I grab her green raincoat and rush out the door, automatically kissing my fingertips and touching the jangling Mezuzah.

Cool rain rolls down my face like a waterfall, drenching me before I reach the first corner. Fearless, I jog, buffeted down the deserted main street. I round the corner of a building and am nearly knocked off my feet by wild, racing winds. The swift-flying raindrops sting sharply, like hundreds of tiny pinpricks. I reach out and cling to a lamppost, keeping my eyes tightly shut. As I brace myself, I peep out between rain-peppered lids. Laughing, giddy, a gray flurry of water and clouds blur my vision. Then, as if laughing back at me, the wind suddenly dies and I nearly fall flat on my face!

I stagger the rest of the way to the store. The only unlocked door is that of Sam and Hys Deli and Grocery. As I *blow* in, fond memories of the tang and salt of Kosher corn beef sandwiches make my stomach gurgle. Barefooted, weirdly garbed humans huddle in the doorway waiting for rescue by auto. We laugh together when the storm-ward side of their rescuing taxi hood blows open. *Bang*!

I purchase two loaves of bread, considered a fair share of the deli store supply. So different from when we bought food for *Rosh Hashanah* (Jewish New Year) and *Yom Kippur*; then there had been an over-abundant supply of everything. Bread in hand, I duck back into the storm to walk five blocks home. I pass a man sporting a bathing suit. A kindred spirit. "Nice day!" he shouts, and splashes on.

Back at the apartment, I hand the dripping bundle to B, then, dart out again to get medicine for Mrs. S., ignoring Bs warnings. The three blocks to Silverman's Drugstore, I walk down the center of the street. Palm fronds and cocoa-nut clusters, torn loose from their moorings, crash to earth inches away from me. I lean forward now and breath in the rain-mixed air that tastes of earth, sea, and charcoal. I choke as if paddling in a choppy sea, gasping for air between swells.

My heart thumps wildly as, through half-blinded eyes, I finally recognize the immediate danger. Expecting to be dashed to death each second, I run the last block, my soaked clothes weighing me down. Dripping buckets, I enter the pharmacy, lit only by dimly flickering candle flames.

"Are the electric wires down?" I ask, befuddled.

"Not yet," the clerk answers. "The company turns off the current in case they do come down." After procuring the essential medicine and catching my breath, I head into the hurricane again. How would a powerless Miami survive?

I'll bet the sea is rough! By taking the long way home, I'll see some wild surf. Drawn by my foolish curiosity, I wrestle past shuddering buildings and bobbing palm trees to the oceanfront. Near the half-submerged sea wall I stand, bracing myself and join the surging storm, terrible and magnificent. Massive breakers barge like ferocious, cage-maddened beasts, crashing against steel and brick. Slithering up buildings, then falling back, they roar and crack upon iron girders, leaping high in cascades of gray, saltine foam. *Boom!* *Sssssss* ...

Gleefully, the tempest spends its fury, swooping down on earth in a devil's mill of black clouds. The wind rips millions of tiny droplets from the sea's surface and spits them through palm fronds, shrubbery, and awnings, leaving everything in its wake in shreds. Wind whistles over the ground, scooping up water and beating down a wide wall of beach sand into the streets, blockading roadways with uprooted trees. Rending asunder everything in its path, the storm releases its pent-up fury. I stand, shivering, pummeled, B's coat flapping wildly against me. I'm motionless in the middle of chaos, and my heart is strangely calm. The violence of the storm expresses the devastation of my grief for my own family and for the Jews ... and brings me peace.

A school-age boy stumbles past me in the wind as I start home. Now, it's easy going! With the wind at my back, I lean into its pressure, my feet more forward than chest, and coast on the winds. Entering a narrow side street, funneled with tall buildings, I pause. Breathless, I stand in the middle of the street watching depressing devastation. I feel small and absolutely helpless in the hurricane's power. Debris flies helter skelter and sends me scuttling to be safer against the buildings. However, sliding along the cold slippery walls doesn't help.

An iron pipe suddenly sags, smashing a huge glass window of Frankel's Cleaners right in front of me. I shrink back, trying to find something on the flat surface to cling to. There is nothing. Off balance, I push on over the jagged glass strewn on the walk. Then it strikes me. This hurricane is God's creation. So why should I be afraid? I relax again and carefully wend my way home, unharmed.

When I return, the S. family welcomes me warmly. B. says she prayed the whole time I was gone. Such love and acceptance comes so unexpectedly, but I relish it. That's the way God often does things, though, I'm learning slowly.

I don dry clothes and eat hot kosher food by candlelight. Sausages, pickles, vegetables, and rich rye bread, basking in the joy of being cherished.

Friday, September 19

This morning, the wind has lost some fury, but some folks, still cautious, continue to prepare. Few places are open for business, and on my way for a swim tonight, I rarely meet a passerby. While romping in the dark waves, six big boys pester me, following me with a spotlight. I finally leave my midnight plunge and pretend to leave the beach. I spend time examining the large variety of dead fish strewn on the sands by the storm, and then resume my swim in the turbulent surf after the boys leave. Some things are only satisfying when done alone.

Saturday, September 20

Genuine calm returns, and I witness the worst part of a tropical storm; the aftermath. *Dig out* is the expression locals use. Miami looks wounded. Sorrowful, I realize the awfulness and endless troubles that the twisting winds bring to humanity. Even so, the miracle remains that only one man is injured in this storm.

Tuesday, September 23

Disasters have a way of putting things in perspective. Disagreements with Mrs. S. seem nothing compared to the battle I'd just seen. A different kind of hurricane comes in the form of a letter from Mom. My dear brother Buddy had been found and locked up again on September twelve, this time in the Pacific Colony in Spadras, California; an institution for the criminally insane. Now, it seems he's labeled *crazy* for running away again. God, I'm helpless to assist my family; Your will be done.

October 31, 1947

I leave Miami Beach. My curiosity is finally satisfied and money is in my pocket again. Older, wiser, and trusting God more than ever before, I'm ready for the next leg of my journey.

CHAPTER 17
Mystery in a Georgia Swamp

November 1947

Curiosity drives me into the Okefenokee Swamp just as it had driven me out into the hurricane in Florida. Past the busy season, there are no tourists hiking the paths or canoeing the waterways as I pedal easily along Highway 84, then turn south to enter the gloom. Not even insects keep me company. Summer heat is gone, but armed with a woolen coat, heavy jeans, and socks, I'll be fine as I head north into winter.

"Baltimore for Christmas," I chant as cool breezes lick my cheeks. My recently re-trained muscles perform their duties with mechanical rhythm as I imagine how I will luxuriate in the warmth of family, surrounded by dozens of relatives I haven't met yet, but who eagerly wait my arrival. Mom would fly to meet me there. Pop and Juney couldn't afford to come.

The swamp looms on my right, an impenetrable dark green. Pooled on either side of the partially paved road, acres of shallow water glisten, stained eerie black by the tannins produced by fallen, decaying leaves. The water smells like burnt earth. I'd read that the swamp water is drinkable, but when I slurp some up, I'm *bitterly* disappointed in its flavor.

My mind wanders as I ride mile after mile. "Thanksgiving

is just around the bend!" I say making my voice sound big to fill the emptiness. I especially miss my family now. Thanksgivings past we would all be sitting around our ample dining room table, in our Sunday best. We smile, treat each other kindly for a change, and eat *Belloff-size* helpings, which means three times as big as that of an *average* serving. Mother made sure the savory turkey, swimming in juice inside its golden crisp skin, always looks like the one on the cover of *The Saturday Evening Post.* There would be sweet, buttery yams and green beans, tangy avocado, and pomegranates so tart they make me grin. Then we would devour flaky-crusted, spicy apple and pumpkin pies that only Pop can bake. After every plate is empty, Mom would ceremoniously clear the dishes and then we'd all pitch in to wash and dry. Every dish spotless and put away, then out would come two decks of cards, and we'd play a cutthroat game of Canasta, Pop's eyes sparkling with delight. We hoped he wouldn't drink too much ...

This year is so different. Buddy would eat turkey at the Pacific Colony. Don and his recent bride had moved to Napa, California, and are too involved in their own lives to make the journey home. Only Juney, Pop, and Mom would be there. I wonder how much they miss me. My heart aches. My stomach growls. I'm grateful for the canned food I bought; for though my map shows towns scattered throughout the swamp, I haven't seen any yet, and I don't know what *swamp people* eat.

Peering closer in the dim light, I spy cypress trees drooping with moss strangling the chokeberry bushes. Pitcher plants, like green and yellow funnels, protrude from the peat that covers the ground everywhere. Budding botanist that I am, I stop to dissect a funnel; sure that no one is looking. There, in the base of the plant, are tiny dismantled bug bodies, proof that the plants eat meat. How disturbing yet awe inspiring that God would create something like this!

The Seminole Indians had named this swamp *Land of the Trembling Earth*. To test this theory out, I jump up and down on the peat, which floats on the surface of the murky water. The trees and bushes shiver and shake, and the swamp seems fragile, in spite of the sturdy cypress trees that tower like giants over me.

The Suwannee River moves slow as a cold snake, beside the road, slithering southwest on its way to the Gulf of Mexico. I would love to see its source, said to be somewhere in the heart of the swamp, but I'm certainly not going to leave the safety of the roadway to look for it. Creatures of the swamp can move very quickly, and I squint into the dense foliage as I cycle, watching for white-tailed deer, black bears, or Anhinga (inedible, web-footed turkeys). Snakes, like an underwater rainbow, flash orange, yellow, green. Others glisten black. The plain brown ones are poisonous moccasins. And there are alligators, like other places I'd been, only bigger. I don't see any fifteen footers, though, thank goodness! Alligators can move very swiftly in a straight line, and I would have to ride a crazy zigzag to avoid one if it decided to pursue me. God, why do you grow such a large variety of deadliness here?

This evening, as I hang my hammock and sleeping roll between two evergreen trees, my ears ache with the quiet, interrupted only by an occasional pounding of a redheaded woodpecker. No cars, no people, for a full day of riding.

However, halfway through my second night here, I wake, startled by men's voices and the glare of headlights shining straight at me.

"Howdy, miss. We've been patrolling the roadway and noticed that you're sleeping outside. Are you all alone?" a man wearing a shiny sheriff's badge asks.

"Yes, sir, but I'm all right. There hasn't been anyone around for days," I reply, trying to be respectful, though barely conscious.

"Well, you should know, it's terribly dangerous for a girl to sleep alone out here unprotected," another man says, blinding me with his flashlight.

"When you get to my town, just down the road, you need to come directly to my office, and I'll find a place for you to stay." The sheriff and his men climb into his car and leave as quickly as they'd come, not waiting for my reply.

My skin crawls. They had seemed friendly, interested in my safety, but at the bottom of the back of my neck a creeping, knowing sense lingers. What secrets do they share? I stash this awareness away and fall into a *half-sleep* for the rest of the night.

Things usually seem less creepy in the daylight. Cycling into the backwoods town soon after the sun rises, I notice that words are misspelled on some of the shabby storefronts. Odd... . Obediently, because he is an *authority*, I find the sheriff's office. The sheriff cheerfully escorts me down the street a few blocks to a one-room cabin that he had *prepared* for me.

"I'm sorry there's no hot water. But, the electric works, and I just put a strong latch on the door," he says, leaning against the rough doorway and eyeing me.

"Thank you, sir. This will be my last night in this area. Tomorrow I plan to head north to Savannah, and I will certainly use that nice lock tonight," I say, forcing a grin.

I explore the tiny town and then look for the St. Mary River, which I'm told flows southeast from the swamp to the Atlantic Ocean. By evening I return to my cabin. The crawling sensation in my neck returns stronger than ever as dark comes to the swamp town. I nonchalantly coast Chariot around to the back of the cabin and park it under the window. If anyone asked, I would say I parked it out of sight so that it wouldn't get stolen. But that's not quite true.

The dusty gingham curtains hanging in the cabin are riddled with holes, so I turn off the light to do my daily bathing in the small sink. Unsure of why, I decide to sleep in my jeans and Pendleton, and even my shoes. I lay awake late into the night. I hear rustling sounds coming from under the house. What kind of swamp critter digs there? I read Psalm 91. It helps me relax.

I'm about to fall asleep when someone knocks insistently on the door. A man's voice says softly, then louder, "I really do need to see you!" His voice booms, and the latch starts to wobble. That's it! I grab a few things already wrapped in a bandana and crawl out the back window like a wild thing. Fear gives me strength; once on my Chariot, I speed quickly into the night without looking back. I escape using only sounds, smells and shadows to guide me to safety through the night. The dark swamp embraces me, protecting me from what I'd left behind.

The fragileness of the swamp reminds me of the fragileness of trust, and that things and people aren't always what they seem or what I wish they were. Who was so violent at the door? It could have been any man. It's like an older memory I try to forget. A drunken man at the door. "God, I pray for whoever it is that they can know you, and be forgiven. And thank you for showing me that when I get the *creeps*, it could be You warning me to keep me safe. Amen."

CHAPTER 18
Epiphany
(An Illuminating Realization)

November 1947

Dear Mom,

    Departed Gainesville, Florida at ten a.m. after delivering a speech to the local press. I splurged last night on a hotel room for one dollar and seventy-five cents. I'm cleaned up; feel nice and fresh now. Today I stopped to eat soup, egg sandwich, and milk at a café and to write this letter. Pine forests and farmland replace the orange groves and swamps of Florida, as I continue north, though there are still plenty of creeks, marshes, and ponds. The wind changed direction, blowing now from the north. My hands are stiff from the winter cold, but my feet feel toasty in my heavy leather shoes. Hope you will have my artic sleeping bag waiting in Savannah, my next stop. Happy Thanksgiving! Love, Norma

The words in my letter ring cold and stark, like the weather. As I drop the letter to Mom in the mailbox, shame creeps then pounces, a predatory animal, and chews on my unsettled mind. Am I to blame for what had happened in the

Okefenokee Swamp? Did I deserve to be put in jail in Pensacola? So often I'm confused about where my responsibility lies. Where do I leave off and others begin? Am I the only human animal with this problem?

Chariot, brave Chariot carries me through another crisp winter day, wheels crunching dry leaves, moving north, always north. Morose, my thoughts sink deeper. I'm an imposter, an impersonator, as surely as the men at the club in New Orleans who try so hard to be women. I'm impersonating a self-created image for the public and for my family. The problem with being an impostor is that one lives in constant fear of being found out! Each time I speak to my admiring public, the same questions.

"Why are you doing it?"

"Aren't you afraid?"

To these questions, I give the same pat answers I think everyone will approve of. And although one part of me actually believes them, another part knows they are only half-true. I say over and over, "I'm seeking a liberal education, getting to know the American people, testing my faith in God, etcetera."

I long to be honest; honesty sets me free. The truth is I'm not a brave athlete looking for an education. In reality I'm running scared from responsibility, from the box being built around me; a box constructed out of everyone's expectations. My parents, my teachers, my brothers, sister, and even Neill all expect something from me, and I can't say *no* to them. Moving myself physically from one place to another, exerting effort through engaging my muscles to get to a new destination—I try to out-distance the box.

However, I can't escape. Mother makes sure that in each large city I visit, reporters are waiting for me—cameras glaring, questions stabbing. Trying to avoid the attention, I no longer call home, writing, sporadically, instead. Still the reporters hunt me down, and, the more famous I become, the larger my shame grows. I don't deserve praise and adoration; I fear shame or pride will devour me. Then, the real Norma Jean Belloff will die ... Only a doll stuffed in a box will be left.

The stories of Mountain Lions begin when I reach Savannah, Georgia, on December third. At each small town gas station or café that I stop, people gasp when I tell them my favorite place to sleep is on the ground in the woods. The farther north I travel toward North Carolina, the more frequent and dramatic the tales of warning about cougars become.

"They meow like a domestic cat, but don't let that fool yer," warns one local.

'They're nearly nine feet long," adds another. "They can leap forty feet, horizontally. Jumping out of bushes onto the back of their prey, the mighty beasts suffocate their meal with one giant bite, breaking the neck. Snap!"

"What should I do then, if I should see one?" I ask, only slightly concerned but wanting to make them feel important. I'd heard about cougar in San Diego, and all the way through western Texas, but still hadn't seen one.

"Don't run away, or play dead. Stare the cat boldly in the eyes, make loud but calm shouting noises, and wave your arms and legs to make yourself seem bigger," answers a weathered backwoodsman. Everyone who lives here speaks with authority. However, when I ask how many people have actually been attacked by mountain lions on the east coast, they answer with vague shrugs of the shoulder and "I don't know."

I read somewhere that white-tailed deer is the mountain

lions' prey of choice, so I determine to appear very un-deer-like while bicycling through the east coast wilderness.

Winter night falls as I continue north on Highway 17 toward Charleston, South Carolina. A half moon rises in the fading dusk, making the gravel on the sides of the road glow white. My eyes adjust, watching for mountain lions and deer.

"I won't get my flashlight out until absolutely necessary, that way conserving batteries that are costly to replace," I say to whatever rustles in the bushes. No worries about snakes, black bears, or alligators, thank goodness; it's too cold for them to be milling about in the road.

Suddenly the wind puffs, and every little shadow becomes a lion ready to pounce on me. If a lion does come toward me in the night, I will stand very still and yell, "All right, go ahead and kill me. However, if you're going to kill me, do it quickly, one giant slash across the throat. Please don't do it slow, because I really hate pain. But, you might want to think twice about killing me right now, because I'm on a mission of self-redemption and my grandmother is expecting me for Christmas in twenty-two days!" Grrrrrrh ...

I realize I've been in a battle since the Okefenokee Swamp, and even long before that. A battle with myself. Truth comes like an invisible warrior to my rescue, soothing my heart and protecting me. While my parents love me with expectations, my Grandmom loves me without any.

I need to go to the source and get to the root of the problem. At Grandmom's God will surely show me how. For now, I lie down in peace, surrendering to another night of frosty bliss, with good memories of Grandmom's soft hugs wrapping around me like a lion skin coat.

Iris Paris

CHAPTER 19
Freedom in North Carolina

December 10, 1947

Calmed and strengthened by my recent epiphany and by a good night's sleep, I bicycle boldly into Wilmington, North Carolina, prepared for the usual cluster of curious and pushy reporters who would ask endless questions and beg me to pose naturally on my Chariot. The sun shines bright and the sky hangs clear after a cold, crisp night. Today I'm a surrendered warrior, full of mercy, riding my chariot on a mission of peace. I'll tolerate the usual questions from the crowd that will form around me. I hope I'm not too crumpled after a night in the woods, for the photos that will surely be printed on the front page of the Wilmington paper this evening.

Surprise! Mother, you must have outdone yourself in making contacts to announce my pending arrival! The crowd downtown is the largest I've seen yet. But they don't gather around me as I arrive in their midst. Instead they cluster around a school bus stopped in front of a school where dozens of Negro children were filing on, supervised by Negro teachers. As the crowds thin around me, I'm not even noticed. I walk Chariot over to address a dignified looking man in a black suit who seems to be in charge.

"Where are they going?" I ask, as he continues to load the children.

He stops loading children and turns to face me. "I am Mr.

S., a teacher from the city of Faison, just north of here. We are taking our students, as well as some from Wilmington, on a trip to see the *Freedom Train* today." He enunciates carefully, perfect southern English, looking me directly in the eyes.

Curious and excited I say, "I'd like so much to see it also. May I ride along with the children?" After all, I reason to myself, I'm on this trip to learn, and I love freedom and I adore trains!

"We have segregation laws in this state that must be followed. I'm sorry but you cannot ride on this bus." He answers, staring at the ground.

I know about segregation well from my travels in the south, but isn't North Carolina in the North? My jaw tenses. "Where does the North begin, then?" I challenge.

"You must remember that Richmond, Virginia, was the capitol of the confederacy during the Civil War, and that is far north of here." He pauses, holding his chin in his hand, and then says, "You could go with me, if I drive my car. My wife is also a teacher and can ride with the students to supervise them."

"Thank you, Mr. S.," I say. Saved again by the mercy of a stranger. Thank you, God. I quickly secure my bicycle inside their school and hop into his waiting vehicle. On the seat between us lay some papers, lesson plans perhaps. Something scribbled big and in red catches my eye. "NAACP supporter Langston Hughes, poet, wrote this."

The Birmingham Station's marked COLORED and
WHITE.
The white folks go left, the colored go right.
They even got a segregated line.
Is that the way to get aboard the Freedom Train?

"You planned your trip just right," Mr. S. says, as he carefully removes the pile of papers and places them on the back seat. "This is the only day the Freedom Train will be in Wilmington. Yesterday it was in Richmond, Virginia, and tomorrow it will be stopping in Columbia, South Carolina."

"So what is the Freedom Train?" I ask.

He explains as he drives, following close behind the school bus. "It is a special exhibit train which has been created to help people remember and appreciate their freedom in this country, now that the war is over. President Truman approved its design, construction, and what it would carry and where it would go. It started in Pennsylvania in September and will eventually visit every state in our United States of America. This is history in the making, and I want my students and my own children to be a part of it."

At the Freedom Train, I wait in line with the Negro schoolchildren, conscious of the glances from white people in the crowd. When one staring woman shakes her head, saying, "Tsk, tsk," I close my eyes and see red. I want to blurt out something mean, but I know it will just fuel an already smoldering fire. Am I the only one who finds it absurd that there are segregation lanes here while waiting to see the *freedom train*? The Freedom Train! What's the point of having it if people can't stand in the line of their choice?

I silently determine that I must talk to President Truman about this. After all, he's the one that created the Freedom Train. He's in charge, isn't he?

Once we're on the special painted, red, white, and blue Diesel Electric Streamliner train, we discover their precious *freight*. Four of the cars contain the original documents of *The Declaration of Independence*, the *United States*

Constitution, the *Bill of Rights*, the *Magna Carta of* 1215, the *Emancipation Proclamation*, and the German and Japanese surrender documents that ended World War II. Also, the actual Iwo Jima Flag. All of these national treasures are guarded by twenty-nine carefully selected Marines, wearing their dress blues. Even so, it seems risky to have so much of our country's history in one place. What would happen if the train derailed or caught on fire?

We stand patiently in line for over two hours for our turn. I chat with Mrs. S. She's petite and comely, but very professional; she invites me to come home and stay with them after the field trip! Her youngest daughter, dressed like a doll in the palest pink with hair in ringlets, jumps up and down in delight at this prospect.

"I'd love to come stay with you in your town, but I have to bicycle there, not ride in a car. It's a promise I made myself from the beginning that I would not accept any rides. Although the weather is brisk, making the offer tempting, I might miss something important." What if I'd missed the Freedom Train!

Hoping not to offend, I promise to stop and see them when I arrive in their town. How dear their whole family is. How blessed I am to know them. I say goodbye back at the school and continue North and slightly West now on Highway 117. Cold all the way, the sun peeks in and out behind storm clouds. By the time I reach Faison, darkness has come and with it frigid rain. I find the lovely, two-story brick house before I become an ice cube.

I knock and Mrs. S. opens the door, swooping me into her dainty arms. "Hm, hm, hm, hm, hm, child," she says. "You're soaked. We've already had supper, but let me heat something up for you. You can stay in the guest room.

Children! Come down and say hi to Miss Norma Jean. She's come to stay with us awhile."

Have I come home? It smells like my own house, the furnishings are familiar, and the sound of children giggling and racing down the stairs reminds me of Buddy and Juney. We decorate their huge Christmas tree, adorning one corner of their stately living room. Even their heirloom ornaments resemble the ones back home.

Mr. and Mrs. S. say the words that my mother can not. "We're *proud* of what you're doing, Norma."

"We *admire* your pioneering spirit."

"Your family must miss you very much."

"I will write to your mother and father as soon as you leave to let them know you are fine, and on your way to Baltimore," Mr. S. promises.

December 14, 1947

Spending two wonderful days with the S. family, I leave now only because I'm afraid I'll miss Christmas at Grandmom's. As it is, I'll have to average sixty miles per day to get there in time. I wonder if I violated segregation laws by staying with a Negro family. If I did, I'm not sorry. It was worth any risk to spend time with such fine people.

The peace and joy of the season fill my heart as I pedal North into the cold, forested, rolling hills of North Carolina onto Highway 301 and then into Virginia. I'm a woman on a mission that I *can* accomplish with God's help.

CHAPTER 20
The Root of the Problem in Baltimore

December 19, 1947

"Over the river and through the woods, to Grandmom's house I go," I sing, shivering as I push on Chariot's ice-coated pedals. Up and down on the hilly streets of Baltimore City I ride. Six-inch snowdrifts twinkle in the evening streetlight; Christmas fills the air. I feel numb from top to bottom, nose so bright I might be *Rudolph*, but with my heart so merry, I could be *Santa*. Uncle Orville's house would be my first stop. His house sits on Highway 301, just two miles south of Grandmom's place.

I zoom through brown street slush across the booming metropolis. Everything is hustle-bustle, bustle-hustle. Noise pummels my icicle ears; sirens scream, horns honk. Chariot maneuvers with no trouble, though occasionally his tires splash unsuspecting sidewalk travelers. Familiar startled looks appear on faces. Why is a young woman riding a bicycle on a cold winter night? Winter-coat-clad people, skin all shades of brown, scurry along the sidewalks, ducking into smelly crab joints, restaurants specializing in boiled crab.

Is this really the North, or is there segregation here too? Before the civil war, Maryland had been part of the South. I learned, while visiting the Freedom Train, that Maryland had also been home to ex-slave and brave freedom fighter

Harriet Tubman during the Civil War and after. She died in her own home somewhere near here, thirty years ago. Nick-named "Ol' Chariot," Harriet fought for freedom for all people. I admire that. I'm fighting for freedom too.

"Moss grows longest on the North side of the tree," Harriet coached hundreds of Negro slaves fleeing to the North and escaping during the night. They say her home provided sanctuary for as many as fifteen refugees at a time. She also fought for women's rights, especially the right to vote. Soon I would be old enough to exercise that right. Thank you, Harriet, for using your life so well. What I wouldn't give to have met her face-to-face and shake her work-worn hand.

"If I could only hug you, Mom. You're so wonderful," I bubble over on the phone when I reach Uncle Orville's a few minutes later. "I stopped here to thaw out and make sure someone will be at Grandmom's to let me in out of the cold when I get there." I chuckle nervously, hearing only steady breathing from Mom's end of the phone. "Are you coming for Christmas, Mom?" I hold my breath in anticipation. Another long pause.

"Norma, I won't be able to make it there in time for Christmas. Financial problems. I need new glasses, and I think I should be here for Buddy. He's having troubles at the *Colony*." My heart sinks like a stone in water. I shiver in spite of the heat from my uncle's roaring fireplace. Mom had promised to come to Baltimore to see me for Christmas. My hopes of earning her love were dashed again! No matter what I did, others were more important. I indulge in another dose of self-pity.

"I understand, Mom," is all I can say, stifling the sobs

tearing at my throat. Silent wet streams roll down my cheeks as I squeeze my eyes tight, trying not to show my hurt to the cluster of relatives standing close to me in the narrow hall while I talk. I'm not surprised—just disappointed. My daily prayers for my mother to love me unconditionally hang in heaven, unanswered, it seems.

A few miles later, I reach my destination. The family home-stead stands close to the crest of the hill on Morrell Park Road, about one mile south of downtown Baltimore. A sub-stantial four-story home built in the late eighteen hundreds, it sports clapboard siding and a long, narrow veranda across the front, complete with wainscoted ceiling and hand-carved railings. Two unique circular windows decorate the fourth floor, center front, and center back of the house. Like huge chameleon eyes, the one in front looks forever south, toward the all boy's college, the other toward the industry-laden downtown and harbor. Grandmom and Pops peek expec-tantly out the frost-covered living room window as I push Chariot up the icy sidewalk to the front door. I'm home.

Christmas finds me spoiled, lavishing in familial love and adulation from my many cousins and aunts and uncles. My huge suitcase of clothes I'd mailed ahead from San Antonio greets me. Most special, a box of oranges and pomegranates arrives, straight from Mom and Pop's garden. I inhale the sweet and pungent scents, and for the moment, am trans-ported back to San Diego, where the temperature would be much milder and the poinsettias outside the kitchen door would be in full bloom. "Try not too think too much about that, or homesickness will spoil everything," I warn myself.

Newspaper photographers knock on our door the day after Christmas and request shots of me and my kin. I resent the intrusion but give them what they want. It's the price one pays for being a *public person*; one's life does not belong to oneself.

The secret to understanding myself is buried in Baltimore. Things change so slowly here that one doesn't notice. Even the spring-fed well that mother scooped water from to quench the thirst of her twelve siblings still bubbles clear in the half-acre back yard. I listen and observe, fascinated by the family history lesson—the history of me!

I learn from my multitude of relatives who have lived in Baltimore all their lives, that Mom and Pop had been neighbors and friends since childhood. Mom had dropped out of high school to help her ailing mother and hard-working father raise her twelve younger siblings.

Father, *the boy next door*, lost both his German-born parents to illnesses when he was just thirteen years old. He worked as a stable boy until he joined the Navy at age twenty. He has one sister, my Aunt Hilda, who lives only a few blocks away.

On returning from one of his submarine assignments when he was thirty-two, Pop noticed Mom in a new way; she had just turned twenty-eight. People say they were an unlikely match. Pop, raised liberal Lutheran, dressed flamboyantly and loved to spend. Mom, raised strict Baptist, was conservative in every way. My parents were living proof that *opposites attract*. And so they began their gypsy life in the Navy, moving from submarine base to submarine base, raising four *Navy Brats* until they retired to *paradise* in San Diego.

Aunt Hilda says I look like Grandmom. How could this be? Like something from a second-hand store, Grandmom dresses daily in her crumpled seersucker pinstripe house dress, button-up-the-front, hem below the knee. She wears her smoky white hair pulled back tight, twisted into an unflattering bun. Gravity is winning, and though taller than me and large all over, her bosoms sag to her waist. She usually wears a frown; the skin around her lips is permanently pursed, as if she were endlessly sucking a straw.

Though Grandmom is only sixty-five years old, she is ailing. She lives in grief, I think. Grieving the loss of her second child in infancy; grieving for sin in the world. I feel weighed down by her sorrow. What does she dream about, or is she too tired to dream? Proverbs 17:22 says, "A broken spirit dries up the bones." Is this what is happening to her? "Life is a veil of tears, Norma," Grandmom says and sighs as we wash dishes together. "Life is serious, Norma," she scolds gently when I share my dreams of changing the world. When I ask her questions that make her uncomfortable she says, "I wonder," or "Whatever is in God's plan," both of which are her ways of ending the conversation.

But when Grandmom wraps her arms around me, I feel her old strength. Safe and protected from the harshness of life, her hug is firm; she gently pats my back and strokes my hair while rocking me back and forth. She lets go of me only when I am ready, giving a rare smile as she inspects my face to see if I'm restored.

Grandmom's spring garden always makes her smile. My mother is the same way, and I too find a singular joy in my garden. Will my children also be like this? By nurturing something and watching it grow, I feel necessary, needed, and hopeful. I think Grandmom's hope is buried in her garden like a treasure, nestled among the roots of her tulips, roses, and weeping wisteria. We tiptoe together daily through her patch of hope and beauty, feeling protected from the harsh realities of life.

Something keeps popping up like a cork; bobbing and sinking, bobbing and sinking in the sea waves of my mind. *Sins of the father are passed to the children*, it says in the Old Testament. Sin has a ripple effect I think, like a stone tossed in a still pond. It reaches out and touches everything nearby. In my Grandmom I see the roots of my own hopelessness. Grown into my mother, it pulls and drags me down also. Generation after generation of our family is rooted in hopelessness. God, I don't want to pass this on! Please let the sin of hopelessness stop with me ... Amen.

Then there's Aunt Ethel, second daughter to be born into the Arnold clan. She doesn't fit the family pattern, and I adore her! Bold and spry, she loves everything about life. She dances, sings, and laughs at everything. Bouncy blonde hair decked with ribbons and bows, nails painted a garish red, she's the living antithesis of all things hopeless. She's a breath of fresh air and a reminder that *life is for having fun*. How has she escaped the legacy of hopelessness? I need to know! Although I want to be close to her whenever she comes to visit, I don't tell anyone. I fear being disloyal to Mother; the punishment would be intolerable shame.

February 15, 1948

Mother finally arrives in Baltimore by train. Her morose mood dampens everyone's spirits. Why has she come? There is strained congeniality, a pretense of familial closeness, but underneath something very different brews. She criticizes my behavior at every opportunity in private, while in the public eye she remains the proud and doting mother.

"What have I done to deserve your disfavor?" I want to ask. When will I ever hear the words out loud, "I'm proud of you, Norma, my oldest daughter?" Am I too much like Aunt Ethel? Are you jealous of me?

Another's resentment and subtle vindictiveness can generate the most painful revenge possible. Anxiety creeps in like an army of biting ants invading my peace of mind, whenever I'm near her. She stays at Grandmom's two weeks and I'm relieved when she leaves. There's the truth. I don't like my mother, and she doesn't like me. How can we ever be close? For now, other people are filling my cup with love. My relatives and my fans give me what Mother can't. Apparently, we don't always get what we want, but we do get what we need, if we ask. I'm glad You're big, God ... Amen.

I haven't dated since Florida. Now, I meet the boy next door, Jimmy. Irish Catholic, attending the local all-boy's college, he captures my heart; I stay longer than I had planned. Between his classes and study, he shows me the sights. Then one last evening fling. We ride the train to Coney Island from Baltimore, dressed in our *Sunday* best. We thrill at the amusement park, a dance pavilion, and a large gold moon. A walk down a country lane walled by wild honeysuckles and roses completes the romance we feel for one another. Though he asks me to stay and be engaged, I say no.

Like the sailors with a girl in every port, I have left a broken heart in every state. After a miserable train ride back to Baltimore, I depart, promising to write, as I had each of the wonderful men I enjoyed before, knowing none of them was *the one* for me.

March 1948

I'm fat! I stare in disbelief at my bloated image in the full-length mirror in the third story bedroom of Grandmom and Pop's house. There's no escaping the honesty of the reflection of my twenty-pound overweight body. What had happened to that svelte, slinky, elegant athlete's figure that I flaunted shamelessly in front of newspaper cameras as I lounged on the beach in Miami? I'd die of embarrassment to be seen in that same swimsuit now. It probably wouldn't fit, like most of my other summer clothes that I've given away to myriad female cousins. How could I change so much in three months? Perhaps I should only have stayed a week at Grandmom's, as I originally planned. But, I had earned money by washing all the windows in the neighborhood, inside and out. I'm not completely useless!

Three healthy meals a day cooked by my doting grand-mother had grown me to this overly ample size. Gram feels it is her duty to fatten up *skinny little things*, and, as usual, I can't say no. Besides, it is family tradition to eat when we are sad, happy, mad, or bored. We eat whenever we gather together. My layers of fat fend off the east coast cold, like a bear hibernating in its den until spring. In addition, because there'd been so many times during this trip when I'd not had enough, I eat to compensate.

But perhaps the roots go deeper. Grandmom told me that my mother had bought the bestseller by Dr. Watson the month I was born, *The Psychological Care of Infant and Child.* Mother thought that someone with a degree from *John Hopkins University* must know better than her. In his book, Dr. Watson suggests an infant's character could be molded by putting her on schedules, which included when and how much she ate from the time she was born. Grandmom said Mother went overboard with this new idea, only to realize her error by the time my sister, June, was born. So only I was a guinea pig of Dr. Watson's theories.

Whatever the reasons, chubby and rested, I mount my shiny new steed, Chariot III. The Lyons Club of Baltimore delivered this gorgeous silver and black racing bike to Grandmom's house on March first. A total surprise and a blessing, they decided to give it to me after I spoke about my trip at their monthly meeting. I must have done something right! I relinquish Chariot II to my Aunt Ruthie, mother's sister who is still in high school, who also has dreams of traveling around the United States.

March 1948

I know it's time to move on, to leave the soft, warm nest that Grandmom provided through the cold Maryland winter. Just as mother robins push their children out of their nests, I need to push on. Perhaps this is a sign of maturity; I don't need someone older and wiser to push me.

I'm headed for my birthplace, New London, Connecticut.

With only two days to get there to celebrate my twenty-first birthday, I know I can do it. So off I speed, waving to a mass of relatives and a few local reporters clustered with flash bulbs as I coast down Morrell Park Hill and toward Highway 1, heading north. A perfect spring day, I feel perfectly okay. I know, now, why I traveled more than three-thousand miles for the last year and a half. I was searching for my identity, and I found it. I'm part of the *Arnold clan*. Nothing more is required; loved and accepted unconditionally, finally, being Norma is good enough. "Thank you, God, for giving me the desires of my heart," I pray as I pedal. "Thank you for setting me free, again."

Chapter 21
Safe Harbor

March 13, 1948

Chariot and I *fly* up Highway 1 and enter New York State with the wild turkeys. Spring sun shining bright, the balmy air thick with sickening sweet cherry blossoms, I get my first glimpse of about fifty wild turkeys, milling and flapping a few hundred feet ahead, in the middle of the straight road I travel. The brown, black, and bronze striped creatures cluck contentedly as both males and females glide ahead of me in a steady stream up and down the gentle knolls that border the road. Cartoon characters, the turkeys have absurdly skinny legs and necks supporting bulbous, feathered bodies in between. The males are spectacular. Sporting four-foot wingspans, huge fire-red waddles and rough, bald heads, their long necks glow bright white. Their red and white snoods dangle flashily, partially obscuring their white beaks.

The turkeys perform a majestic, graceful ballet in the privacy of the woods, and my heart dances with them, a mirror of my newfound feelings of acceptance and belonging. I no longer feel like the *ugly duckling*. The flock of fifty or so turkeys suddenly take flight. One by one—flutter and glide, flutter and glide, like giant brown moths—they hover a few feet off the ground then float single file toward a gurgly rain-gorged creek.

When I tell my story to some *locals,* they are surprised
to hear that the turkeys are back. The wild Eastern Turkeys
had mysteriously disappeared from New York State years
ago, they say. I laugh at the irony of it all. Clearly, God, you
are in control! I praise you ... Amen.

Ever since I was a kid in school, I dreamed often of seeing New York, the *King* of all American cities. *Whoosh.*
Whoosh. Almost before I know it, I reach the heart of the
city. Sun still shining, temperatures in the seventies, the
streets are choked with traffic as I follow the Boston Post
Road. America's original east coast highway; it was built in
the 1600s to provide a route for mail delivery from Florida
to Maine.

Up onto the George Washington Bridge I ride, arch-
ing over the mighty Hudson River. Halfway across I stop,
gasping as I take in the impressive array of buildings making up the composite part of New York, from the Bronx to
Wall Street. I stand here and watch the teeming metropolis
surge. Pompous, puffing tugboats chug along the river, pulling graceful steamers. A few cargo vessels labor upstream.
On either side of the Hudson, the city squeezes the water-
way tight, choking it with docks, warehouses, and boats.

Riding along close to the curb, feeling waffled by the cars
and trucks that rush along through the city streets, suddenly,
I hear a masculine voice. "Hello, there." Must be my imagination. I glance around. The voice sounds very near.

"I said, hello there!" Riding directly behind me, on a
sleek racing bike is a pleasant-looking, middle-aged man,
dressed in jeans, tennis shoes, and a tan corduroy shirt. I pull

to the curb and stop abruptly. "I've been riding behind you for several blocks. Your load fascinates me," he says, pulling to a stop beside me. "I try to keep my bike as light as possible. You seem to be trying to make yours as heavy as you can. Strange," he adds, smiling knowingly.

"Well, I'm touring on my bike and you're just out for a jaunt," I reply, trying not to sound too defensive. "I'm headed for Connecticut, Washington D.C., and then back to California."

"That's quite a journey, you know. Most professional bicyclists I know wouldn't even try such a trip." He continues.

"Maybe not," I counter, "but I made it from California to New York, so I'm sure to make it home again."

"Let me shake your hand." He says, gripping mine firmly when I acquiesce.

"Why?" I question, impatient now to continue on my way.

"My name is Otto Eisele. Perhaps you've heard of me. I'm past president of the American Bicycling League. Right now, I'm training youngsters for the Olympic Trials. I was hoping I'd be the first one to welcome you to New York City." His voice could charm a snake. Wonder how he'd heard about me, wonder what he wants. "Let me give you my address," he continues, handing me his business card with his address scribbled on the back. "If you're going to be in New York a few days, I'd like you to meet my wife and two sons. Besides, I know lots of people who'd enjoy meeting you," he finishes.

Before I could say thank you, he shouts, "Be careful in this traffic, won't you? Bye," and darts off to join the endless stream of city sojourners. He must have read about me in the Baltimore paper. I promise myself to contact him on my way back from Connecticut. What could it hurt? After

I complete my present mission, to be in New London, my birthplace, on my twenty-first birthday.

Olympics? God, what do you have planned for me?

Chariot and I take refuge in Central Park for a good night's sleep. I feel safe in this forest; an oasis of nature in the middle of an *asphalt jungle*. Then, with a tail wind aiding me, I pass through the Bronx, Mount Vernon, and on north to New Rochelle. Crossing the state line, following Highway 1, I enter Connecticut.

Steep, narrowly winding roads to New London are more up than down and wind alternately between the coast and inland. No huge vista from the tops, just trees and more hills. I sing "The Bear Went over the Mountain" more than once as I move swiftly toward my destination. The ride back south will be a coasting frenzy! Wheeee!

The sea towns, salt marshes, and small brightly sanded beaches cuddled by low cliffs and rock rubble contrast nicely with the organized beauty of farms and graceful forest-clothed mountains. The barns, houses, and sheds sit orderly and clean amid plowed or planted fields that seem perfect for a postcard. Picturesque country!

I span the one-hundred thirteen map miles from New York to New London in one day! The temperature dips from seventy degrees in New York to fifty degrees in New London. The foliage changes from fully leafed trees to mere swollen bark. Leaves in New York create lacy shadows, while in New London there are still only shadows of bare branches.

March 14, 1948

New London, full of American history, still looks barren brown with only a light spattering of evergreens on the rolling hills. Even though I know no one in New London, on my twenty-first birthday, the newspaper reporters find me as Chariot and I wander the streets; they ask me to pose in front of strategic businesses in the old downtown area. I inform the curious crowds that I was actually born near the Submarine Base in Groton, which lay on the far side of the newly constructed Gold Star Bridge, which traverses the mouth of the Thames River.

As I camp near the foot of the fort at the gaping mouth of the Thames, I reflect on many things. What is my responsibility to my family? I read the New Testament more since my stay at Grandmom's, looking for hope and a future. I want to be a positive ripple spreading love outward on the still pond of life.

I read a scripture, now, while sea gulls scream and careen in a brisk spring breeze, full of the smell of sea salt. Philippians 2:4. "Look not every man on his own things, but every man also on the things of others." Could this be *sacrificial love*? Caring for someone else more than myself. Crying over and over and loving anyway. Refusing to give in to emotional withdrawal. Refusing to run away, even though it seems unbearable to stay. I must admit, this notion is new to me, but if I'm to create a positive ripple in my family and the rest of the world, I'll need to forgive and give and give and give. Lord, please show me how ... Amen.

March 15, 1948

I bed down for the night south of town, nestled under a clump of pine trees in the middle of a farmer's field. Dar finds me here. Dar is short for *Darn it, that stray puppy just won't go away.* I've never had a dog before. The big brown eyes staring trustingly out from the shiny, coal black head and body capture my heart completely. I have no idea how to care for a growing puppy, so I feed her whatever I eat. She seems content as long as she's near me, so I keep her. She's actually good company when I'm sleeping out in the woods, and I cherish the sense of safety she provides. Is this breaking my rule that I have to do this whole trip alone? I decide that since she isn't human, she doesn't count.

March 16, 1947

Sometimes life is insane, but still glorious. Dar sits up alert in Chariot's basket after I give away a few of my clothes to make room for her; she's worth the sacrifice. She brings me pure joy as we bounce along where ever we go. She doubles my fun, as her ears flap in the fresh sea breezes, her little tail thumping in time to the bumps in the road.

But what will I do with her when I return to Baltimore? A *great idea* hatches. I think Pop needs a pet, and Dar would be perfect. I could ship her home to him, a token of my love and desire to be a part of his life. A token of my forgiveness. A *sacrifice of love*. I could just imagine Pop strolling down the board walk of Ocean Beach, his faithful dog by his side. How proud he would be, and how loved he would feel by me, his oldest daughter.

With my new plot fueling my flight, Chariot, Dar, and I head back to Baltimore to carry out my plans. Visit Washington, D.C., mail Dar to my Pop, and talk to Otto about the Olympics before I start my long trip home.

CHAPTER 22
Epilogue

Norma stopped to visit Otto Eisele, as he had requested, on her return trip to Baltimore from New London. During this visit, Otto proposed, not an invitation to the Olympics, as she had anticipated, but a challenge to represent the American Bicycling League to establish a Women's Cross Country Bicycling Record. Reluctant at first, Norma eventually agreed, wooed by the New York bicycle team and Olympic trainees.

She received one-hundred fifty dollars for a three-minute radio interview with Bill Stern at Radio City, downtown Manhattan. She also appeared on the CBS television production *We the People* and signed autographs at local department stores. Otto wanted publicity and notoriety. Norma needed financial aid for her return trip. Together they committed to thousands of people to establish a record. Norma felt small, but was expected to accomplish something great! She knew she could do it only with the help of God.

❄

Norma's father gave her permission to ship Dar to him as a gift. However, Dar contracted distemper. Norma spent all the money she had earned washing windows while in Baltimore to try to save the sweet puppy. In the end, Dar had to be put to sleep. "It was one of the hardest things I had ever had to do," she wrote to her father.

In the humid heat of April, Norma rode Chariot III into Washington D.C., just in time for the Cherry Blossom Festival. She had two goals—spend time in the Library of Congress and meet President Truman. She began by spreading out her sleeping roll on the White House lawn, planning to camp out until the President arrived. The friendly security guard who greeted her suggested she would do better if she contacted California Congressman Mr. Downey to assist in getting an appointment with President Truman.

Norma obediently sought out Mr. Downey in his office across the street. He kindly took her under his wing and pursued her dream with her. She stayed for days, checking in each day to see if he had acquired her appointment. While hanging out in her favorite haunt, the Library of Congress, Chariot III was stolen. The news media got a hold of the story and within a few days, her bike was found, dumped but intact in a nearby vacant lot.

Norma slept each night in a graveyard nearby, along with the ticks and poison oak, lying under berry bushes to avoid the rain and waking each morning to the sharp twitter of bright red cardinals. Once she almost broke her leg when it sunk into a soggy grave past her knee.

On the morning of April twenty-seventh, Norma received heartbreaking news. When she checked in with Downey's secretary at about ten a.m., Norma was informed that her appointment with the President had been one hour earlier. They had not known where to find her to let her know. They were sorry and offered to try again. She was sorry and so humiliated that she left town immediately.

By early June, while at the Youth Hostel Headquarters in New York, Norma purchased all the gear necessary for her record try. On June twenty-third she started her trip in front of the Manhattan City Hall, where reporters, officials, bicycle fans, and well-wishers were waiting to see her off. The starter gave her the signal, and she was on her way. Draped across her back hung a white oilcloth sign that said *New York to San Diego.*

Her trip proved fun, but hard work. Pedaling an average of seventy miles per day gave her time to reflect and to dream. She realized she had absorbed the tension of the people on the east coast, and she relaxed as she moved west, chasing the fiery orange ball of sun setting over the Appalachians and each range after that. She often continued riding deep into the night, flashlight illuminating the road, running on the adrenaline that comes from exerting one's will and the excitement of knowing she would soon see all the people she loved the most.

At least forty times a day her nerves were blasted by friendly horns; while she enjoyed the attention, every time she stopped for breaks, she was barraged with questions, which slowed her progress across the USA.

During Norma's trip, she developed painful muscle camps in her legs; she knew she would never make it unless she rested and had her legs massaged. Consequently, she stayed in Arizona for a week to renew her health before continuing.

On August fifteenth, she checked in at the Los Angeles City Hall, then headed south on Highway 101. At La Jolla

Junction, she found most of the town of Ocean Beach waiting for her, including a Motorcade from the Ocean Beach Chamber of Commerce. Horns tooted and sirens screamed as person after person shook her hand. A motorcycle officer led the triumphant procession through La Jolla and Mission Beach to her home in Ocean Beach, California. Norma, so happy that she laughed and cried all the way, waved at her admiring fans until her arm ached. She was home.

When Norma arrived home, she realized what a really wonderful person her mom was. While Norma was racing across the country, her mom had been in the hospital undergoing a major operation. Her mother came close to death, yet her instructions to the family had been to not tell Norma because she thought it would spoil her daughter's trip. Her mother came home from the hospital the day after Norma arrived, to make a complete recovery. Norma stated to the Press, "I shall always thank God for the myriad of blessings which have been mine. I am safely home. The best moments of all, though, were hugging Dad and kissing Mom."

After Norma's return to San Diego, she tried to find the rhythm of the world where she had lived. She dreamed of writing a book, finishing college, and traveling to Mexico and South America. Instead, just three weeks later, San Diego sent her and her racing bike by train to Kenosha, Wisconsin, all expenses paid, to represent California in the Women's National Bicycle Races. Norma took third place.

Norma fulfilled another dream and met plain-spoken President Truman in San Diego in September 1948 as he rode the "Magellan" train on his whistle-stop campaign to be elected. The Press teased the President and Norma about how she had stood up their date in Washington DC and said that the President had come to San Diego just to see her. President Truman replied, "You go right ahead and tell'em that's why I came!" Norma decided he was a likeable man. So did the majority of the voters, who elected him two months later.

Norma attended San Diego City College, then married Berdine Harold Rogers, a geologic engineer who loved the outdoors as much as she did. They cycled up the coast to San Francisco for their honeymoon. They had two children, Blake and Iris. Norma never rode a bike again. She remained a full time homemaker until her death.

Norma's younger brother, Buddy, joined the Navy. He later became a successful businessman and eventually a minister, specializing in helping the homeless in San Diego.

Norma's older brother, Don, married and went to work for NASA, creating computer programs for rockets. He and his wife had one son.

Norma's sister, June, married, had three children, and continued her education to earn a Ph.D. in Psychology.

Norma's father retired from teaching and continued inventing things for the family to use around the house and yard. He stopped drinking during her bicycle trip.

Norma's mother ran a day care, tended her garden, and proceeded to lavish unconditional love on her grandchildren; the kind of love she was unable to express to Norma.

Norma wrote during her trip,

Sometime about five or ten years from now, if you should happen to see a bicycle with a side-car attached wheeling down a highway, slow down and wave ... it will probably be me and a couple of offspring, I hope. I hope. But whether I can go with them or not, I want my kids to learn firsthand, as I did, what a gorgeous hunk of the earth's surface they were lucky enough to be born on and what good people most Americans are.

When I grow old, I hope I remember that there are endless adventures for the mind and soul after youth and physical powers are gone. A person need never be at a 'useless age' if one keeps striding ahead spiritually and mentally, so I believe. I hope the time comes that I can see for myself, because such satisfaction comes from proving true what I am preaching, by practicing it successfully!

Someone once told me that we all carry around in our heads pictures, dreams of what our life is supposed to be like. They suggest it is a great secret of humanity that none of our lives look the way we thought they would, created as they are by our repeated reactions to our circumstances.

I can't tell you how much I disagree with this depressing theory of life. I choose, instead, to rely on the thousands of promises found in the Bible, New and Old Testament. They teach me a very different reality. One of my favorites is in Jeremiah 17:7. Blessed is the man that trusteth in the Lord ... he shall be as a tree planted by the waters. Therefore, I try to look beyond my circumstances, good or bad, and choose to see that God is unlimited and can define my life anyway he wants; He's not limited by dull human imagination.

God's humans are by far the most amazing of all his creatures.

I found that there was good in everyone as I was invited into people's homes all the way across the country and who helped me when I needed it. Perhaps by doing this, I found something that most of us are looking for but never quite find.

Bibliography

Adventures of Tom Sawyer. Selznick International Pictures, Inc. United Artists Release. 1938.

Along Came Jones. A Cinema Artists Production. International Pictures, Inc.1945.

Angel on My Shoulder. United Artists Release. Producer by Charles R. Rogers. 1946

"An Introduction to the Okefenokee." *http://www.okefenokee.com/intro.htm Okefenokee Pastimes.* Accessed, May, 2006.

Belloff, Norma. Journals, letters, and newspaper articles from 1946–1948.

Bentley, Judith. *Harriet Tubman.* New York: Franklin Watts, 1990.

Bultman, Bethany Ewald. *New Orleans.* Oakland, California: Fodor's Travel Publications, 2000.

Krug, J.A., and Drury, Newton B. *Carlsbad Caverns National Park: New Mexico.* Chicago: United States Government Printing Office, Department of the Interior, 1945.

Cerf, Bennett. *Try And Stop Me.* New York: Simon and Schuster, 1945.

Eddy, Lucinda. *"War Comes to San Diego." The Journal of San Diego History.* Winter-Spring 1993, Vol. 39, Numbers 1–2. San Diego Historical Society.

Fabulous Texan. Republic Entertainment, Inc.1947.

Henretta, James. A., David Brody, and Lynn Dumenil. *America, a Concise History.*
Boston, Mass: Bedford/St. Martin, 2002.

"Lecture Notes on John B. Watson." http://www.sonoma. edu/users/d/daniels/Watson.html. Accessed, 7 -3–07.

MacLeod, Fiona. *The Sin Eater and other tales and Episodes*. Chicago: Storen Kimball, 1895.

Naylor, Horey. *Essential New Orleans*. Trento, Italy: The Automobile Association, 1992.

"National Velvet." Metro-Goldwyn-Mayer. 1945.

"Texas City Disaster." http//en.wikipedia.org/wiki/. Accessed, 7–29–07.

The Bluebird. Twentieth Century Fox. 1940.

The Holy Bible. King James Version, 1611. New York: American Bible society.

The Wizard of Oz. Metro Goldwyn Mayer. 1939.

Winston Dictionary for Schools. Chicago: John Winston Company, 1936.